Leisure Manager's Guide to Budgeting and Budgetary Control

by

Simon Shibli

Leisure Manager's Guide to Budgeting and Budgetary Control

Published by Longman Information & Reference
Longman Group Limited, Westgate House, The High, Harlow,
Essex CM20 1YR, United Kingdom.
Telephone: (01279) 442601
Facsimile: (01279) 444501

First Published 1994

A catalogue record for this book is available from the British Library

ISBN 0-582-23906-0

Typeset by Phoenix Photosetting, Chatham, Kent
Printed in Great Britain by Page Bros. Norwich

Contents

Chapter 1
Putting budgeting into context

Objectives

The purpose of this chapter is to show budgeting in the overall management process rather than as a discrete accountancy exercise. Having read the chapter you should have a basic grasp of the following points:

(i)   The importance of budgeting and budgetary control in leisure;
(ii) A realisation that people and communication are an integral part of the budgeting process;
(iii) How budgeting, as a management accounting exercise, relates to financial accounting.

Why has this manual been written?

This manual has been written because there is very little existing material on budgeting and budgetary control in leisure. What does exist, tends to concentrate on the strategic aspects of budgeting as part of the planning process. Whilst this is useful, it does not help the practising managers to understand and perform the day to day operational parts of their jobs better. Interviews were conducted with practising leisure managers before writing started. The results of these interviews were very revealing and have been incorporated into the manual. We found enthusiastic and committed managers who were almost crying out for information that explained budgeting concepts in simple terms. A further refinement was a realisation of the need to use practical examples to illustrate the basic points. The interviews were concluded with the question: "Would you buy a book which covered the principles which we have just discussed?" The most inspirational answer was: "Yes – but please keep it simple".

The manual has deliberately not been written in a prescriptive manner. It is not our role to tell you what you should be doing. A more appropriate role is to realise that budgeting as a component of management accounting must be specific to its own context. What works for First Leisure PLC is unlikely to be suitable for a local authority leisure centre. Therefore, the contents of this manual have been written in such a way as to illustrate how the basic principles can be applied. Hopefully, managers will read the examples and then see how they could be used in their own situations. To reinforce the flexibility of the principles, we have deliberately not included any exercises at the end of chapters. However, there are some questions which invite readers to focus on their current practices and information requirements. The approach to adopt is to evaluate how your own practice differs from basic principles and to try and explain why. This will identify the changes which are needed should you wish to implement any of the principles discussed.

It is hoped that the contents of this manual will be seen as a continued source of reference for managers as they tackle different parts of the budgeting and budgetary control process. In years to come, it will be very satisfying to see dog-eared and coffee-stained versions of this manual, i.e. proof that it has actually been used!

What is the need for budgeting and budgetary control in leisure?

Budgeting is an integral part of the planning process and can be said to represent the objectives of an organisation expressed in monetary terms. Implicit in this statement is the need for plans and their financial consequences to be compatible. This means that financial considerations and the setting of tight, clearly focused objectives is of paramount importance. In the private sector objectives are normally quantitative and simple, e.g. a given level of profit. In the public and voluntary sectors objectives have often been vague, e.g. "encouraging participation". There is a new culture of accountability and providing value for money in the not-for-profit sector. This is perhaps best demonstrated by the introduction of compulsory competitive tendering (CCT) for the management of local authority sports facilities. This requires managers to have a greater understanding and competence in finance generally and in budgeting in particular. Whether we agree with these changing conditions is largely irrelevant since we are forced to live and work with them.

From a positive point of view, leisure is a long-term growth sector of the economy and can provide considerable opportunity for those who work in it. By understanding budgeting and budgetary control principles, it is possible to transfer skills from sector to sector and to have an interesting and rewarding career. The opportunities for managers without reasonably honed financial management skills are severely limited.

People and communication in budgeting

Much of the way this manual has been written focuses on the numerical dimension of budgeting. However, it is worth stating from the outset that the mechanics of budgeting should not be divorced from the human dimensions of participation and communication. Throughout this manual any techniques which are suggested are done so on the basis that managers are aware of the importance of participation in budgeting and also that they communicate their intentions clearly.

For each of the three recognised sectors in leisure there tends to be a hierarchy or chain of command. Typical examples are illustrated in Table 1.1.

A universal problem which often defeats budgeting before its benefits can be realised is that sectors introduce a "top down" budgeting approach. Instances of this include some of the following examples.

- Private sector - directors threatening to close or sell a venue unless managers achieve a predetermined level of profit. This clearly does not involve those who are responsible for meeting the targets and creates an oppressive uncooperative working environment.

Private Sector	Public Sector	Voluntary Sector
Board	Committee (Politicians)	Trustees
Divisional Managers	Chief Officers	Chief Executive
Area Managers	Officers	Managers
Managers	Managers	Staff
Staff	Staff	Volunteers

Table 1.1

- Public sector – grants or subsidies being reduced on political rather than logical grounds. This would force, say, a leisure centre management to reappraise the make up of their programme without being consulted. The net effect is to create a divide between politicians and the people whom they employ.

- Voluntary sector – trustees changing objectives without reference to the financial consequences or collaborating with staff. This would totally undermine any business and financial plan that may already exist.

The limited empirical research available consistently indicates that a "bottom up" approach to budgeting is typically more successful than "top down". Members of the hierarchy are far more likely to be committed to a budget if they have been involved in the planning stage rather than having targets imposed on them indiscriminately from on high.

If a "bottom up" approach is adopted, then there is a greater likelihood that those who are responsible for meeting the targets will consider them to be fair. This increases the probability of the relationship between what is possible and what is required being compatible.

The second aspect of the human dimension to budgeting is the need to motivate people to achieve the goals which have been set. This is perhaps the most difficult task of all because it requires a commitment at all levels to the goals of the organisation. Two techniques which can help in the motivation phase are: firstly, giving feedback; and, secondly, using proper appraisal methods rather than judging people solely on actual versus budget comparisons.

Feedback is one of the most underrated motivational devices available. If members of staff are doing a good job, then they should be told. If things are not going to plan, then some appropriate constructive feedback can be beneficial to getting performance back on track.

Budgeting works most successfully when it is an integral part of a manager's range of skills rather than being a number crunching exercise.

Budgeting as a necessity

Regardless of how desirable it may be to implement budgeting and budgetary control, it must always be remembered that budgeting is not compulsory. Budgeting is a management accounting technique. This means that it is a part of a series of commonly used techniques which provide information in monetary terms to help managers make decisions. The important words here are "commonly used" which illustrate the optional nature of budgeting. This contrasts with financial accounting which is compulsory and requires organisations to report their financial successes and failures in a specified format.

The discretionary nature of budgeting should not be seen as an excuse to avoid budgeting as it is impossible to plan without considering the financial implications. However, if an organisation is required by law to produce certain financial information, then it makes sense that the systems for producing financial and management accounts are compatible. This is illustrated in the next section.

Financial and management accounting – how budgeting fits in

All leisure organisations are required to account for their financial performance. This ranges from large multi-national companies, such as Bass PLC, that are listed on the stock market and who account to thousands of shareholders, to village sports clubs who account to their membership at annual general meetings.

Regardless of the size of an organisation, the financial (or statutory) accounts are presented in a common form, i.e. profit and loss account, balance sheet and cash flow statement. The starting point in quantifying a budget is to understand what these statements are and how they relate to one another.

The fundamental piece of logic that underpins the whole of financial accounting is the balance sheet equation that is expressed below:

$$\begin{array}{ll} & \underline{\text{ASSETS}} \\ - & \underline{\text{CREDITORS}} \\ = & \underline{\text{CAPITAL}} \end{array}$$

Stated in its most simple terms, the balance sheet equation means that those things that are of value to an organisation (ASSETS) minus that which is owed to others (CREDITORS), equals the net worth (CAPITAL) of the business.

An obvious example of the balance sheet equation in practice is a mortgage that we might take out on a house. Imagine a case in which a person has bought a house for £43,500, paid for by a deposit of £7,500 and a mortgage of £36,000. Assuming that the house owner can sell the house for the cost price, then the house owner's balance sheet for the house would be as follows.

	ASSETS	HOUSE	43,500
−	CREDITORS	− MORTGAGE	− 36,000
=	CAPITAL	= NET WORTH	= 7,500

The balance sheet equation should be learnt as shown above because it is the format in which the vast majority of published accounts are presented, i.e. the vertical format. Whatever way the balance sheet is presented (either vertical or horizontal), its meaning is the same and equates to the balance sheet equation.

By understanding the balance sheet equation, it is now possible to illustrate the three financial statements and examine their relationship to one another. The examples shown in Figure 1.1 have been adapted from the accounts of the Phoenix Arts Centre, Leicester from the accounts for the financial year 1991/1992.

INCOME & EXPENDITURE ACCOUNT		BALANCE SHEET STATED AT 31ST MARCH 1992			CASH FLOW STATEMENT AT 31ST MARCH 1992	
INCOME	£s		1992 £s	1991 £s		1992 £s
Leicester City Council	327100					
East Midlands Arts	59089	TANGIBLE FIXED ASSETS	3289	3206	INCREASE IN CASH	13547
Leicestershire County Council	2650					
Arts Council of Great Britain	5977	CURRENT ASSETS			FUNDED BY:	
Ticket Revenue	143733					
Other Income	42380	Stock	2261	2004	OPERATING ACTIVITIES	
Interest Receivable	14028	Debtors	16947	25759	Operating Surplus	3026
Dance Festival	40213	Cash	129507	115960	Depreciation	5855
Trading Sales	66703				Increase in Stock	-257
			148715	143723	Decrease in Debtors	8812
Total Income (net of VAT)	701873	CREDITORS			Decrease in Creditors	-18409
					Increase in Liabilities & Charges	20458
EXPENDITURE		Creditors Payable < 1yr	-64514	-82923		
Trading Expenses	51510				Net Cash Flow From Operations	19485
Salaries and Wages	231666	NET CURRENT ASSETS	84201	60800		
Premises	56240				INVESTING ACTIVITIES	
Supplies and Services	66853				Purchase of Fixed Assets	-5938
Marketing	63891	TOTAL ASSETS minus				
Artist Fees & Film Hire	182832	CURRENT LIABILITIES	87490	64006		
Depreciation	5855				Net Cash Flow From Investing	-5938
Provision for Renewals	40000	Creditors Payable > 1yr				
		Liabilities & Charges	-79498	-59040		
	698847	TOTAL NET ASSETS	7992	4966	NET CHANGE IN CASH	13547
Surplus on Ordinary Activities	3026					
Accumulated Fund Brought Forward	4966	RESERVES (CAPITAL)				
Accumulated Fund Carried Forward	7992	Accumulated Fund	7992	4996		

Figure 1.1 Financial Statements for Phoenix Arts Centre 1991/92

The profit and loss account (P&L)

The first point to note here is the terminology used for the profit and loss account. Leisure organisations in both the public and voluntary sectors do not normally exist to make a profit. Therefore the term "profit and loss" is not an appropriate description of the financial events that have taken place. To counter this, the profit and loss account is also known by some of the following terms: "income and expenditure account", "revenue account" and "expenditure account". Whatever the terminology used, the meaning of this financial statement is the same in all sectors.

The profit and loss account (or other title) is simply an analysis of how the capital of an organisation has changed over a given period. When there has been an increase in capital, a profit (surplus) is said to have been made. When there is a decrease in capital, a loss (deficit) is said to have been made. Using the table above, it is clear that the Phoenix Arts Centre generated a surplus of £3,026 during 1991/1992 and thus its reserves (capital) increased accordingly by this amount.

The components of the profit and loss account are all of those financial transactions which alter capital, i.e. capital increasing items and capital decreasing items. Capital increasing items are incomes such as box office sales, grants, sponsorships and bank interest. Capital decreasing items are expenses such as wages, premises costs, office supplies, artists' fees and marketing.

There are three important concepts under which profit and loss type statements are prepared:

1 Components of the profit and loss account

Only items which affect the capital of an organisation are included. This means that the purchase of fixed assets (e.g. buildings, vehicles, stocks) is not included on the profit and loss account. As an example, if a sports centre buys a new sunbed for £5,000, all that has happened is that one asset (cash) has been exchanged for another (equipment). Assuming that the sunbed is worth £5,000, then the balance sheet equation has not been altered and, therefore, nor has the profit and loss account.

2 The accruals or matching principle

The profit and loss account is prepared under the accruals or matching principle. This means that all income and expenditure must be included in the financial period to which it relates. Many leisure organisations take payment in advance of a service being sold, e.g. hotels and holiday companies. Under the accruals principle, income is not recognised as being a sale until customers receive what they have paid for. Although we pay for our holidays ten weeks in advance, in accounting terms the holiday company can only say that a sale has been made on the first day of the holiday, i.e. when the sale of a holiday has "matured".

On the expenditure side, the accruals principle requires us to record invoices received as expenses even though we have not paid for them yet. For example, when the electricity bill arrives, even though we do not pay it immediately, it should still be recorded in the accounts in the period to which it relates.

To help to understand the accruals concept we need to redefine our understanding of the terms "income" and "expense". An income is not necessarily the receipt of cash but simply an increase in capital. Therefore, sales which are billed for by invoice are a form of income even though we have not received payment for them. An expense is not necessarily parting with cash but simply a reduction in capital. Therefore, receiving an invoice from a creditor is an expense even though we have not parted with any cash.

3 The reporting of non-cash transactions
The profit and loss account includes items that do not involve the movement of cash, e.g. depreciation. Taking the sunbed example above, if we decide that the sunbed has a useful life of five years, then we need to reduce the value of the sunbed over the period of its useful life. In this case, we could depreciate the sunbed at a rate of £1,000 per year for five years. The point to note here is that the cash left the business when we paid for the sunbed and we are simply reducing the value of the asset on paper using the depreciation charge. Intuitively, we know that a three year old car is worth less than the brand new equivalent. The difference in values is explained by depreciation which is a non-cash transaction.

In budgeting and budgetary control, the profit and loss account is the most commonly used financial statement to compare what is actually happening with what was planned to happen.

The balance sheet

The balance sheet is a list of the assets, the creditors and the net value of an organisation's capital at a given point in time. From our example above, if the Phoenix Arts Centre was to be wound up on 31st March 1992, then once all the creditors had been paid, the net worth of the company would be £7,992.

The balance sheet gives a picture of the overall (cumulative) financial position of an organisation and is the most important of the three financial statements. Balance sheets include the transactions which are excluded from the profit and loss account, such as asset and creditor transactions.

Using the balance sheet it is possible to explain how companies which appear to have been profitable on the profit and loss account can become bankrupt, e.g. profits made are insufficient to clear accumulated losses. Equally, they can enable us to understand how other companies can make losses on the profit and loss account and still continue trading, e.g. a strong balance sheet with plenty of reserves.

Revenue spending and capital spending
Understanding what a balance sheet is and how it relates to the profit and loss account provides us with the basis for making the distinction between revenue transactions and capital transactions.

Revenue transactions are those which affect the profit and loss account and are typically transactions which are involved in the day to day running of a business, e.g. wages, rents, rates etc. Revenue expenditure can be generalised as being expenditure on goods or services which are of use to an organisation for less than one year. Revenue expenditure also includes small items of equipment that will probably be of use for more than one year but are not worth recording as assets (capitalising). Therefore, if we pay £500 for an electricity bill, neither the electricity nor the money used in paying for it are of any future use to an organisation. Similarly, if we spend £100 on a typewriter it is probably not worth recording as an asset. Revenue type expenses are said to be consumable.

By contrast, if a sports centre were to buy a new multi-gym, it is likely that the multi-gym would be of value for at least several years. Expenditure on significant items that will be of value for more than one year is said to be capital expenditure.

Capital items are of relatively long term value to an organisation and are commonly known as fixed assets. Examples include buildings, fittings and equipment. Under the matching principle, the cost of capital items is offset over their estimated useful life by depreciation. Capital items have their value recorded on the balance sheet to reflect that they are of ongoing value to a business.

The vast majority of transactions at unit level tend to be revenue rather than capital transactions. This is the underlying reason why in practice the profit and loss account is generally regarded as being the most important.

The cash flow statement

The importance of cash to an organisation is often likened to the importance of blood to the human body. The cash flow statement is an analysis of how the cash available to an organisation has changed during a given trading period. The important point to note is that profitability (a measure of how much capital has changed) does not equal liquidity (a measure of the amount of cash an organisation has available to it). Thus, if a business makes a profit of £10,000 it does not necessarily mean that the business has an extra £10,000 in cash to spend.

The cash flow statement provides a link between the opening balance sheet for a financial period, the profit and loss account for the period and the closing balance sheet at the end of the period. In Figure 1.1, the Phoenix Arts Centre accounts showed a surplus of £3,026 but the cash available to the business increased by £13,547. The difference in profitability and liquidity is explained by three factors: firstly, the purchase and disposal of fixed assets is not shown on the profit and loss account; secondly, the accruals basis of accounting; and, thirdly, the inclusion of non-cash transactions (depreciation) on the profit and loss account.

In practice, the cash flow statement is the least used of the financial statements. The main reason for this is that unit managers are often not responsible for the overall management of cash. In the private sector most cash dealings are carried out centrally, i.e. Head Office decides when to pay creditors and signs the cheques.

In the public sector the cash flow of a leisure centre is a small part of a council's overall cash flow position and is also controlled centrally. However, in the private and voluntary sectors where some leisure organisations are self-contained (e.g. charitable trusts such as theatres or single unit businesses such as an independent cinema) cash flow and its management are essential skills. Many businesses which appear to be profitable often fail because of poor cash flow.

The link in practice

Clearly, there is a considerable amount of work involved for any organisation to meet its statutory financial requirements. Remember that financial accounting is what organisations are required to carry out by law. Budgeting, by contrast, is not compulsory.

Budgeting is one of the disciplines contained within management accounting which can be loosely defined as: "a collection of commonly used business techniques that provide information in monetary terms to assist managers in making rational decisions".

What is important in any finance system is that the management and financial accounting systems are integrated, i.e. the information which meets audit requirements also enables managers to make rational decisions on a day to day basis.

If we use good practice in financial planning, then it can be seen that management and financial accounting systems should integrate. Figure 1.2 below shows the relationship between some of the stages of the planning cycle and the type of accounts that are typically used at each stage.

Planning	Management Accounting
Operating	Financial Accounting & Management Accounting
Reporting (Public)	Financial Accounting
Reporting (Internal)	Management Accounting
Controlling	Management Accounting

Figure 1.2

The only way in which we can realistically meet all of the stages of the planning cycle is to have systems which are based upon the same sets of data.

Example

Consider the staff salaries and wages bill for a swimming pool. In the financial accounts the salaries and wages would probably be reported as a single line as shown below.

Expenditure Account	Actual
Salaries and Wages	125,000

All this tells managers is the aggregate amount spent on salaries and wages. What would be more useful would be a breakdown by type of staff, the amount paid to them and some indication of whether expenditure was as planned. Thus, in a management accounting format the data might appear as in Table 1.2.

Expenditure Account	Actual	Budget	Variance	(U)/(F)
Salaries and Wages:				
Senior Manager	25 000	25 000	0	–
Duty Managers	30 250	30 000	250	(U)
Senior Lifeguards	24 600	25 000	-400	(F)
Attendants	29 500	29 875	-375	(F)
Technical Staff	14 000	13 450	550	(U)
Overtime	1 650	3 000	−1 350	(F)
Totals	125 000	126 325	−1 325	(F)

Table 1.2

(U) and (F) are shorthand for "unfavourable" and "favourable" respectively. They are important in identifying the direction of a variance. In the example above we have used *Actual* minus *Budget* to calculate the *Variance*. Thus a minus figure in the variance column indicates an underspend and, therefore, a favourable variance.

The two points of note here are: firstly, that the management accounts agree with the financial accounts, i.e. the £125,000 in both cases; and secondly, we can see immediately where the sources of the variances are.

With the knowledge that the expenditure on salaries and wages is £1,325 below budget, we can attempt to explain it. In this case, the net underspend of £1,325 can be almost wholly accounted for by keeping overtime expenditure below budget. Managers would also be advised to look at the £550 overspend on technical staff. The explanations and resultant actions arising from the data are relatively simple – all that is needed is accurate information from which to make them.

Summary

Having read this chapter you should be clear about the following:

(i) Understanding working definitions of the three financial statements, i.e. profit and loss account, balance sheet and cash flow statement. It may be helpful for you to prove these definitions to yourself using sets of accounts that you are familiar with. See if you can demonstrate with your own data how the three statements link together;

(ii) Understanding the distinction between revenue expenditure and capital expenditure. For your own organisation or one that you are familiar with, identify examples of revenue and capital expenditure. What is the average proportion of revenue transactions to capital transactions?;

(iii) Understanding the link between financial and management accounting.

Review and management applications

At the end of each chapter there are several questions which ask you to apply what you have just read to your own work context. The questions are designed to enable you to see how management principles can be applied in practice. Equally the questions will also identify some of the constraints which will need to be negotiated prior to the principles being used.

(1) How is the budgeting process conducted in your organisation?

(2) To what extent is participation at all levels and clear communication an integral part of this process?

(3) What financial reports are currently produced in your organisation? Divide this into management accounting data and financial accounting data.

(4) In an ideal world, what data would you like to be produced?

(5) To what extent is the reality short of what you would really like?

Further reading

Henry, I.P. (ed) (1990) "Financial Management and Leisure Provision" Chapter 4 of *Management & Planning in the Leisure Industries*, MacMillan, London, pp 97–126.

Wilkinson-Riddle, G.J. and Barker, B.E. (1988) *Accounts Trainer for the IBM PC and compatibles*, Pitman, London.

Tilley, C. and Whitehouse J. (1992) *Finance and Leisure*, Longman/ILAM, Harlow.

Chapter 2
Types of budget and budgeting techniques

Objectives

The objective of this chapter is to illustrate both the types of budget which leisure managers will typically encounter and to examine the process by which budgets should be put together. This will place budgeting as an integral part of the planning process rather than being an isolated number crunching exercise. The key learning and discussion points are as follows:

(i)   To show and discuss the various types of budget and introduce the integrated budget;

(ii) To appraise the commonly used budgeting methods;

(iii) To show how budgeting can act as a check for internal consistency.

The various types of budget

1 The profit and loss account budget

The starting point for putting together a budgeted profit and loss account is to be aware of the objectives. Managers should ask themselves the following question: "What exactly do we wish to achieve in financial terms?" The answers will vary depending upon the sector in which a manager is working, but typical examples are represented in Table 2.1.

Private Sector	Public Sector	Voluntary Sector
A return on capital of 15%	To break even	To operate within the resources allocated
£50,000 net profit	To meet the terms of a CCT contract	
Last year's profit plus 6%	A recovery rate of 75%	

Table 2.1

With the knowledge of the financial objective(s) of any business plan, it becomes possible to begin constructing a budget to see if the objectives are possible in monetary terms. Alternatively, managers can predict what needs to happen in order to make the stated objectives and their financial implications compatible.

The major point about the budgeting process is that it allows managers to simulate events in advance of them happening so that they know what the business essentials are and what to concentrate on. There is little mileage in not budgeting and then being surprised to discover that everything has gone hideously wrong after the event!

The best way to illustrate the financial mechanics of the budgeting process is by use of a practical example.

Example

The manager of a ten pin bowling facility has been asked to compile a profit and loss budget for the forthcoming year. Head Office has told him that the facility is worth £250,000 and that they are looking for a return on capital of 12%, i.e. £30,000 profit. Last year's budget for the ten pin bowling facility is summarised in Figure 2.1.

Total Admissions	52,000	
	£s	
Entrance Fees	31,200	(60p per head)
Shoe Hire	26,000	(50p per head)
Bowling Fees	130,000	(£2.50 per head)
Cafe Income	46,800	(90p per head)
Total Income	234,000	(£4.50 per head)
Cost of Sales	65,000	(£1.25 per head)
Salaries	24,000	
Wages	52,000	
Premises	21,000	
Supplies	12,000	
Marketing	32,500	
Total Expenses	206,500	
Net Profit	27,500	(the bottom line!)

Figure 2.1

To achieve the required return, the manager will need to increase profits by £2,500 or just over 9%. Note how the expression "the bottom line" is derived from financial statements. There are three ways in which the net profit can be increased in theory:

(i) By increasing turnover and keeping expenditure at the same level. As an example, the manager could try to increase the number of admissions or alternatively increase the prices charged to customers;

(ii) By decreasing expenditure and keeping turnover at the same level. As an example, the manager could reduce expenditure on marketing and hope that the same number of people continued to use the facility;

(iii) A combination of both (i) and (ii), i.e. increasing turnover and decreasing expenditure simultaneously. As an example, prices could be increased and the number of staff hours reduced.

Whatever method is selected to manipulate the bottom line to the required outcome, the decision should be based on rational information about the business – preferably from marketing research.

For the sake of simplicity in this example, we will assume that the facility is not operating at maximum capacity and that it would be possible to accommodate more customers. Additionally, we will assume that an increase in admissions will not lead to an increase in any of the costs other than the cost of sales. How many more customers would be required to increase the net profit to £30,000?

Possible solution

We know that the average customer spends £4.50 when using the facility and that the costs involved in generating this sum are £1.25. This tells us that the gross profit (or contribution) per customer is £3.25, i.e. £4.50 minus £1.25. We also know that we need to generate another £2,500 worth of additional profit. Therefore, the number of additional admissions required simplifies down to:

$$\frac{\text{Additional profit needed}}{\text{Gross profit per customer}} = \frac{2,500}{3.25} = 770 \text{ extra admissions}$$

This can now be tested on the budget, as shown in Table 2.2.

A simple example like this is fine for illustrating a point but it only shows one dimension of the budgeting process, i.e. it only tells "how much". What managers also need to help them manage effectively is precisely "when" incomes and expenditures will occur. The "when" part of the budgeting process is illustrated in the next section.

2 The expanded profit and loss account budget

The timing of income and expenditure flows is an important concern because most leisure provision is subject to seasonal variations. For example, sports centres are busier in winter than in summer and holiday resorts are busier in summer than in winter. These sorts of factors need to be considered when constructing a budget. In the example of the ten pin bowling budget, the fact that there were 52,000 admissions in the year does not necessarily mean that there were 1,000 admissions per week.

Total Admissions	52,770	
	£s	
Entrance Fees	31,662	(60p per head)
Shoe Hire	26,385	(50p per head)
Bowling Fees	131,925	(£2.50 per head)
Cafe Income	47,493	(90p per head)
Total Income	237,465	(£4.50 per head)
Cost of Sales	65,963	(£1.25 per head)
Salaries	24,000	
Wages	52,000	
Premises	21,000	
Supplies	12,000	
Marketing	32,500	
Total Expenses	207,463	
Net Profit	30,002	

Table 2.2

From a managerial and control point of view, the budget needs to be divided into subsections so that we can be aware of the operational and financial implications of the level of business and therefore manage rationally. In practice this means that we should divide a financial year into at least monthly subsections.

Developing our original example further, consider how the monthly profit and loss account would look if the pattern of admissions was as laid out in Table 2.3.

Month	Admissions
April	4,000
May	4,300
June	3,700
July	3,500
August	3,000
September	3,600
October	4,000
November	4,500
December	6,000
January	5,500
February	5,200
March	4,700
Total	52,000

Table 2.3

In the interests of simplicity, this example assumes that the only items that vary in proportion to the number of admissions are the income per head and the cost of sales per head. All other costs are assumed to be constant for each month. Even with this basic example we can see how much the amount of profit varies according to the level of business at different times of the year. See Figure 2.2.

	April 4000	May 4300	June 3700	July 3500	August 3000	Sept. 3600	Oct. 4000	Nov. 4500	Dec. 6000	Jan. 5500	Feb. 5200	March 4700	Total 52000
ADMISSIONS													
INCOME													
Entrance (60p)	2400	2580	2220	2100	1800	2160	2400	2700	3600	3300	3120	2820	31200
Shoe Hire (50p)	2000	2150	1850	1750	1500	1800	2000	2250	3000	2750	2600	2350	26000
Bowling (£2.50)	10000	10750	9250	8750	7500	9000	10000	11250	15000	13750	13000	11750	130000
Cafe (90p)	3600	3870	3330	3150	2700	3240	3600	4050	5400	4950	4680	4230	46800
Total Income	18000	19350	16650	15750	13500	16200	18000	20250	27000	24750	23400	21150	234000
Cumulative	18000	37350	54000	69750	83250	99450	117450	137700	164700	189450	212850	234000	
EXPENDITURE													
Cost of Sales (£1.25)	5000	5375	4625	4375	3750	4500	5000	5625	7500	6875	6500	5875	65000
Salaries	2000	2000	2000	2000	2000	2000	2000	2000	2000	2000	2000	2000	24000
Wages	4333	4333	4333	4333	4333	4333	4333	4333	4333	4333	4333	4337	52000
Premises	1750	1750	1750	1750	1750	1750	1750	1750	1750	1750	1750	1750	21000
Supplies	1000	1000	1000	1000	1000	1000	1000	1000	1000	1000	1000	1000	12000
Marketing	2708	2708	2708	2708	2708	2708	2708	2708	2708	2708	2708	2712	32500
Total Expenditure	16791	17166	16416	16166	15541	16291	16791	17416	19291	18666	18291	17674	206500
Cumulative	16791	33957	50373	66539	82080	98371	115162	132578	151869	170535	188826	206500	
PROFIT/LOSS	1209	2184	234	-416	-2041	-91	1209	2834	7709	6084	5109	3476	27500
Cumulative	1209	3393	3627	3211	1170	1079	2288	5122	12831	18915	24024	27500	

Figure 2.2: Ten pin bowling alley example

Using the 12-monthly budget format, the manager can see immediately that there are certain implications for the efficient running of the facility. Examples include:

(i)   The facility experiences peaks and troughs in the level of its business. It may be a good idea to match resources such as staff hours to the peak times and to reduce staff hours during the summer;

(ii) From July to September the facility is running at a loss. This is the time to be either trying to promote the venue or to save on expenditure. Alternatively, this may be the period in which to schedule maintenance, i.e. while the facility is quiet;

(iii) The winter months are the most profitable. Therefore it makes sense to have sufficient staff and working equipment available to cope with the level of business.

These sorts of decisions cannot be made on the basis of the annual summaries, and indicate the importance of breaking budgets down into manageable and meaningful sections.

Budget periods

The most commonly used timespans in which to break down budgets are either by calendar month or by lunar month. Lunar months divide a year into 13 four weekly cycles. The basic point about making comparisons is the need to be comparing like with like; comparing a February in a leap year with 29 days and four weekends with a March that has 31 days and five weekends would not be comparing like with like. A brief appraisal of each method's advantages and disadvantages is outlined in Table 2.4.

Calendar Month Advantages	Lunar Month Advantages
A year is divided into commonly recognised timespans.	A year is divided into equal periods enabling better like with like comparisons.
The 12-month cycle makes half-yearly comparisons possible.	Greater control is possible because 13 financial reports are produced rather than 12.

Calendar Month Disadvantages	Lunar Month Disadvantages
Months do not contain an equal number of days; the variation ranges from 28 to 31.	The four-weekly cycle concept is not understood as readily as the 12-monthly cycle.
Months do not contain the same number of weekends, e.g. some four others have five.	Quarterly and half-yearly comparisons are difficult to make.

Table 2.4

Other periods can also be used, including fortnightly and weekly. No one way is better than another. The best budget timespan to select is the one which is the most appropriate to fulfil the information and control requirements of the management.

3 The budgeted balance sheet

Unfortunately, the budgeted profit and loss account does not tell us everything we need to know about a business. As has already been stated, profitability does not equal liquidity, i.e. the fact that the ten pin bowling alley has made a profit of £27,500 does not mean that Head Office has another £27,500 to spend. An example of how the capital could have changed is illustrated in Figure 2.3.

Clearly, it can be seen that the profit of £27,500 has been accounted for by increases in fixed assets, reductions in current assets and reductions in long-term borrowings. Therefore, to help complete the picture of what happens during trading, we need to construct a budgeted balance sheet as in Figure 2.4. Although the figures used are fictitious note should be made of how the monthly changes to the balance sheet are the same as the monthly profit or loss summaries from the profit and loss account.

	Opening Balance	Net Change	Closing Balance
TANGIBLE FIXED ASSETS			
Building	300 000	20 000	320 000
Equipment	80 000	10 000	90 000
Total Fixed Assets	380 000	30 000	410 000
CURRENT ASSETS			
Stocks	10 000	2 000	12000
Debtors	5 000	2 500	7500
Cash	25 000	−25 000	0
Total Current Assets	40 000	−20 500	19 500
CREDITORS <1 YEAR			
Trade Creditors	21 000	−3 000	18 000
Taxes	4 000	−1 000	3 000
NET CURRENT ASSETS	15 000	−16 500	−1 500
TOTAL ASSETS minus CURRENT LIABILITIES	395 000	13 500	408 500
CREDITORS >1 YEAR			
5 Year Loan	20 000	−4 000	16 000
Mortgage	125 000	−10 000	115 000
TOTAL NET ASSETS	250 000	27 500	277 500
CAPITAL			
Share Capital	100 000	0	100 000
Profit & Loss Account	150 000	27 500	177 500
TOTAL CAPITAL	250 000	27 500	277 500

Figure 2.3 Ten Pin Bowling Balance Sheet

	Opening Balance	April	May	June	July	Aug	Sept	Oct	Nov	Dec	Jan	Feb	March	Net Change	Closing Balance
TANGIBLE FIXED ASSETS															
Building	300000	−1000	−1000	−1000	9000	−1000	−1000	10000	−1000	−1000	9000	−1000	0	20000	320000
Equipment	80000	0	0	0	0	0	0	0	2000	2000	2000	2000	2000	10000	90000
Total Fixed Assets	380000	−1000	−1000	−1000	9000	−1000	−1000	10000	1000	1000	11000	1000	2000	30000	410000
CURRENT ASSETS															
Stocks	10000	200	0	0	−250	−300	−400	300	500	800	300	400	450	2000	12000
Debtors	5000	350	−200	100	−300	250	400	−100	500	400	500	350	250	2500	7500
Cash	25000	−591	1634	−116	−9400	−1241	159	−9241	584	1259	−5966	109	−2190	−25000	0
Total Current Assets	40000	−41	1434	−16	−9950	−1291	159	−9041	1584	2459	−5166	859	−1490	−20500	19500
CREDITORS <1 YEAR															
Trade Creditors	21000	−250	−250	−250	−534	−250	−250	−250	−250	−250	−250	−250	34	−3000	18000
Taxes	4000	−1000	0	0	0	0	0	0	0	0	0	0	0	−1000	3000
NET CURRENT ASSETS	15000	1209	1684	234	−9416	−1041	409	−8791	1834	2709	−4916	1109	−1524	−16500	−1500
TOTAL ASSETS minus CURRENT LIABILITIES	395000	209	684	−766	−416	−2041	−591	1209	2834	3709	6084	2109	476	13500	408500
CREDITORS >1 YEAR															
5 Year Loan	20000	0	−500	−1000	0	0	−500	0	0	−1000	0	−1000	0	−4000	16000
Mortgage	125000	−1000	−1000	0	0	0	0	0	0	−3000	0	−2000	−3000	−10000	115000
TOTAL NET ASSETS	250000	1209	2184	234	−416	−2041	−91	1209	2834	7709	6084	5109	3476	27500	277500
CAPITAL															
Share Capital	100000	0	0	0	0	0	0	0	0	0	0	0	0	0	100000
Profit & Loss Account	150000	1209	2184	234	−416	−2041	−91	1209	2834	7709	6084	5109	3476	27500	177500
TOTAL CAPITAL	250000	1209	2184	234	−416	−2041	−91	1209	2834	7709	6084	5109	3476	27500	277500

Figure 2.4 Ten Pin Bowling Monthly Balance Sheet

The budgeted balance sheet for any month can now be calculated, e.g. the planned position for the end of September would be the opening balance for the year plus or minus the changes in the columns April to September inclusive. This forms the basis of comparison for what actually happened compared to what was planned to happen.

However, there is the possibility that by not budgeting for cash properly, what was planned to happen and what actually happens do not coincide.

4 The budgeted cash flow position

The most significant concern when looking at the budgeted balance sheet is realising the importance of budgeting for cash. Without sufficient cash to meet the day to day requirements of a business it will inevitably fail. By budgeting for cash, managers will have a clear idea of when there are likely to be cash flow problems. By being aware of potential difficulties, such as running out of cash, remedial action (control) can be exercised, such as rescheduling payments or organising overdraft facilities to avoid running out of cash.

Opening Cash Balance	25 000
Closing Cash Balance	0
NET CHANGE TO CASH	−25 000
Funded by:	
OPERATING ACTIVITIES	
Operating Surplus	27 500
Depreciation	12 000
Increase in Stock	−2 000
Increase in Debtors	−2 500
Decrease in Creditors	−3 000
Decrease in Taxes	−1 000
Net Cash Flow from Operations	31 000
INVESTING ACTIVITIES	
Purchase of Fixed Assets	−42 000
Net Cash Flow from Investing	−42 000
FINANCING ACTIVITIES	
Reduction in 5 Year Loan	−4 000
Reduction in Mortgage	−10 000
Net Cash Flow from Financing	−14 000
NET CHANGE TO CASH	−25 000

Figure 2.5 Ten Pin Bowling Budgeted Cash Flow Statement

Many managers are not required to manage the cash flow position of their operations because cash flow is managed centrally. However, if at some point in their career a manager becomes self-employed, involved in a management buy out or in charge of a self-contained major event, cash flow management will be essential. Budgeting for cash is relatively straightforward and involves realising the timings of actual inflows and outflows of cash.

The starting point is examining how the cash available to a business has been planned to change and what the consequences of this are. This is illustrated best by examining the overall budgeted cash flow position of the ten pin bowling facility and also a monthly cash flow forecast. See Figure 2.5.

As with the balance sheet example discussed earlier, all that the budgeted cash flow statement has told us is "how much" the cash position has changed and not "when". To be fully in control of cash available, the budgeted cash flow needs to be broken down into smaller segments so that a more detailed analysis of cash changes can be seen, e.g. on a monthly basis:

Again, this is a simplistic example and is based on the following assumptions:

(i)   All income and expenditure for each month has occurred on a cash basis. In the real world it is unlikely that this will be the case;

(ii) Depreciation is charged at £1,000 per month giving an annual total of £12,000. Thus in effect the purchase of fixed assets is the net increase of £30,000 plus the depreciation charge, giving a total of £42,000 for the year.

The major point to realise is how the three financial statements link up to one another, as in Figure 2.6.

	April	May	June	July	Aug.	Sept.	Oct.	Nov.	Dec.	Jan.	Feb.	March	Totals
Opening Cash Balance	25000	24409	26043	25927	16527	15286	15445	6204	6788	8047	2081	2190	
Closing Cash Balance	24409	26043	25927	16527	15286	15445	6204	6788	8047	2081	2190	0	
NET CHANGE TO CASH	–591	2225	–116	–9400	–1241	159	–9241	584	1259	–5966	109	–2190	
Funded by:													
OPERATING ACTIVITIES													
Operating Surplus	1209	2184	234	–416	–2041	–91	1209	2834	7709	6084	5109	3476	27500
Depreciation	1000	1000	1000	1000	1000	1000	1000	1000	1000	1000	1000	1000	12000
(Increase)/Decrease in Stock	–200	0	0	250	300	400	–300	–500	–800	–300	–400	–450	–2000
(Increase)/Decrease in Debtors	–350	200	–100	300	–250	–400	100	–500	–400	–500	–350	–250	–2500
Increase/(Decrease) in Creditors	–250	–250	–250	–534	–250	–250	–250	–250	–250	–250	–250	34	–3000
Increase/(Decrease) in Taxes	–1000	0	0	0	0	0	0	0	0	0	0	0	–1000
Net Cash Flow from Operations	409	3134	884	600	–1241	659	1759	2584	7259	6034	5109	3810	31000
INVESTING ACTIVITIES													
Purchase of Fixed Assets	0	0	0	–10000	0	0	–11000	–2000	–2000	–12000	–2000	–3000	–42000
Net Cash Flow from Investing	0	0	0	–10000	0	0	–11000	–2000	–2000	–12000	–2000	–3000	–42000
FINANCING ACTIVITIES													
Reduction in 5 Year Loan	0	–500	–1000	0	0	–500	0	0	–1000	0	–1000	0	–4000
Reduction in Mortgage	–1000	–1000	0	0	0	0	0	0	–3000	0	–2000	–3000	–10000
Net Cash Flow from Investing	–1000	–1500	–1000	0	0	–500	0	0	–4000	0	–3000	–3000	–14000
NET CHANGE TO CASH	–591	1634	–116	–9400	–1241	159	–9241	584	1259	–5966	109	–2190	–25000
CASH AVAILABLE	24409	26043	25927	16527	15286	15445	6204	6788	8047	2081	2190	0	

Figure 2.6 Ten Pin Bowling Monthly Budgeted Cash Flow Statement

In practice, the timings of cash movements rarely match the budgeted financial statements. As an example, consider the case of a dual-use swimming pool which is open to the public and also used by schools. Typically, the public pay in cash and schools are invoiced on a monthly basis. The revenue tends to be 75% from public usage and 25% from schools usage. Under these conditions the financial statements for three months in which revenue was £4,000, £6,000 and £8,000 respectively would appear as in Tables 2.5 and 2.6.

Profit and Loss Account				
Income	Month 1	Month 2	Month 3	Total
Public Swimming	3,000	4,500	6,000	13,500
Schools Swimming	1,000	1,500	2,000	4,500
Total	4,000	6,000	8,000	18,000

Table 2.5

Cash Flow	Month 1	Month 2	Month 3	Month 4	Total
Public Swimming	3,000	4,500	6,000	0	13,500
Schools Swimming	0	1,000	1,500	2,000	4,500
Total	3,000	5,500	7,500	2,000	18,000

Table 2.6

The same principle is true for expenditure items. For example, venues which run licensed bars probably receive an invoice for stock delivered on a weekly basis. However, it is unlikely that these invoices will be paid until a month later. To offset the effects of timing differences it is advisable to construct a cash flow budget which concentrates solely on the actual movement of cash, i.e. inflows and outflows as in Figure 2.7. In practice the cash flow budget is simply an extension of the swimming pool example above applied to every area of income and expenditure.

The advantage of this approach is that it illustrates clearly the cash consequences of a proposed course of management action. If what is planned to happen indicates areas of difficulty, such as running out of cash, managers are then in a position to make sensible decisions to avoid this. On a positive note, if cash surpluses are identified by projections then they can be used to earn interest for the periods in which they are not required.

In practice, the cash flow projection is a subjective process and requires managers to know their business well and to base their forecasts on sound assumptions.

An example includes policies such as the control of creditors and debtors. If a manager budgets to have invoiced sales paid within one month, then it is essential that payment is made within this time. This can be ensured by sending out a statement, issuing copy invoices or gentle persuasion by telephone.

CASH INFLOWS		April	May	June	July	etc.
Sales						
Grants						
Other Income						
Total Inflows	A					
CASH OUTFLOWS						
Cost of Sales						
Wages and Salaries						
Premises						
Supplies						
Services						
Marketing						
Other Expenses						
Capital Expenditure						
Total Outflows	B					
NET INFLOW/(OUTFLOW)	A−B					
OPENING BALANCE	C					
CLOSING BALANCE	D					

Figure 2.7 Budgeted Cash Inflows and Outflows

The integrated budget

It is unlikely that one person will have sole responsibility for policy formulation, the writing of a business plan and the setting of budgets. Normally, these duties are the responsibility of several people or departments within an organisation. Therefore, it is important that those people who are responsible for budgeting do not make their plans in isolation of what is happening elsewhere in the organisation. As an example, the manager of a sports centre should not be planning on increasing the number of people using the swimming pool without regard to extra pool attendants required and the cost of a marketing campaign to attract more customers.

There are two dimensions to an integrated budget – internal consistency and integrated components.

1 Integrated in terms of internal consistency

The budget is the overall plan expressed in monetary terms; thus, it is implicit that prior to a plan being implemented it should be tested to see if it works. Clearly there is little point in proceeding with a plan and budget that do not give the required outcome.

This can be modelled by looking at a typical budget cycle and the practical steps that should be taken at each stage.

The budget cycle

Stage 1: define your objectives
What exactly do you plan to achieve?

This will be a statement of the overall outcomes that are required and this naturally depends on the sector and type of business that is being considered. Examples include a net profit requirement, ROCE, recovery rate or net expenditure.

These are the sorts of decisions that are usually taken by managing directors or leisure services committees.

It is highly advisable that objectives are ranked into some order of priority. If the objectives prove to be inconsistent with the financial outcomes, then modification can be made and the higher priorities can be protected.

What services are going to be provided and at what cost?

Who are they targeted at and what is the time scale?

Stage 2: audit of resources
In order to achieve stage 1, what level output is required and what resources are needed to deliver the output?

This is a check to see if an organisation has both the assets and human resources to meet the practical implications of the objectives. It is not possible for a swimming pool to increase its opening hours if extra staff are not available, nor is it possible to budget for 2,000 admissions to a health suite if it has not been built yet.

The audit of resources should be carried out at unit level by senior management in consultation with heads of department. The result of this consultation will lead to the compilation of the fixed assets budget.

Stage 3: operational strategies required
What are the practical implications of meeting the objectives?

The budgeting cycle is now becoming focused on practical day to day issues. These include considerations such as the balance and range of the programme of services offered, opening hours and pricing policy.

As in stage 2 above, this should be carried out by senior management and heads of department.

The difference between the objectives and the operational strategies can be summarised as: the objectives are a statement of where an organisation would like to be, and the operational details are the courses of action that will enable them to get there.

Stage 4: allocation of responsibilities
Who is going to do what and by when?

All tasks need to be divided into discrete measurable units which encourage accountability. There is little that is more frustrating than jobs not happening because of the perennial excuse "I thought so and so was in charge of that". The most effective way of achieving the allocation of responsibility is by managers committing themselves to written action plans. This is essential in removing any ambiguity in knowing precisely who is responsible for delivering what and by when.

This is the responsibility of all staff, but in practice is led by managers and heads of departments (HODs). The process of consultation and agreement to strategies and responsibilities requires a participative approach. When we refer to decisions being made by HODs and managers, it is implicit that this is done after consultation with those staff who are affected by the resulting decisions.

Stage 5: preparation of budgets
What are the results in financial terms of the agreed plan?

The written detail and agreed policies can be translated into monetary terms of "how much" and "when". In practice, this is by the construction of a budgeted profit and loss account and balance sheet.

Under integrated conditions, HODs should prepare budgets for their areas of responsibility. In a leisure centre this may mean separate budgets for "wet" side, "dry" side, marketing, private lettings and trading operations. These departmental budgets can then be consolidated into one overall or master budget.

The integrating of departmental budgets into the master budget is the responsibility of the senior management in collaboration with a finance officer, accountant or treasurer's department.

This is the first opportunity to check whether or not the plan and its financial implications are consistent. If, for example, the profits or the recovery rates are too low, then revision and modification of the proceeding stages will be required. This highlights the importance of ranking priorities.

In reality there are five ways in which a budget can be modified to create consistency with the objectives:

(i) *Increase in income*: turnover targets can be increased, such as more admissions than originally budgeted for or greater sales per head from the budgeted number of admissions. In the not-for-profit sector, funding bodies could agree to provide more subsidy in order to enable the full range of objectives to be met. Alternatively, new initiatives could be undertaken such as the introduction of trading operations.

(ii) *Decrease in expenditure*: where possible, savings can be identified that will improve the bottom line without altering the objectives. This does, of course, imply that an organisation is not working as economically as possible and that savings can be made.

(iii) *Increase in income and decrease in expenditure*: the two options above are not mutually exclusive and it is possible in theory to implement both simultaneously.

(iv) *Modify the financial outcome required*: this involves accepting the consequences of the budgeted outcome and revising financial expectations accordingly. Naturally, the likelihood of this depends upon the magnitude of the difference between what was required and what has been budgeted to happen. It also depends upon the financial health of the organisation and its ability to survive a financial reversal.

(v) *Modify the objectives*: it is also possible to realise that the objectives may be too ambitious given the resources available. The course of action available here involves either reworking the objectives or omitting those which are of the lowest priority until a satisfactory outcome is achieved.

The key point of the various solutions is that the process occurs rationally by the making of sensible decisions which are agreed along the full chain of command rather than irrationally or politically.

When an acceptable solution has been arrived at, it is necessary to construct a budgeted cash flow to check that the organisation will not run out of cash or, if it does, that overdraft or other borrowing facilities can be arranged well in advance of when they are needed.

Stage 6: approval of budgets

The importance of the approval of budgets is that once a budget has been approved, it then becomes a directive against which the performance of those who are responsible for achieving it can (in part) be judged. The only really effective way that this can be implemented is through the use of a participatory budgetary process rather than setting budgets by imposition. The integrated approach to approval is to agree the components of the budget with those it affects as the individual components of the budget are put together.

Approval of the budget at the highest level is a form of protection for those who are required to work to it, in the sense that they know precisely what they need to achieve in terms of financial performance.

In terms of consistency, a budget which has been put together in a participatory manner and approved at the highest level means that everybody concerned is working to the same agenda or "singing off the same hymn sheet". One of the commonest reasons for budgets not working is individuals or departments not sharing the same objectives as the organisation as a whole, or working to sub agendas.

Stage 7: implementation of budgets

Once approved, budgets can then be implemented formally. The key criterion at this stage is that the budget must have been constructed, approved and be ready for implementation prior to the start of the financial period for which it is intended. In the event of a budget being implemented retrospectively, it implies that the organisation has been operating without a proper plan during the period in which the budget was not approved.

Stage 8: measurement of performance

To what extent are we achieving what we set out to achieve?

Budgeting and control are dynamic processes that do not cease once the budget has been implemented. It is only possible to discover how well you are doing by receiving feedback. This means receiving regular information which reports what has actually happened compared to what was planned to happen and where necessary a detailed analysis of the variance.

The key requirements for effective measurement and reporting of performance have two vital components:

(i) *Accuracy*: all reporting must be accurate, which implies the use of efficient procedures for data collection and a systematic approach to the reporting of financial information.

(ii) *Timely*: to be able to react to the implications of financial data, managers need information quickly. There is no reason why data from daily returns and weekly banking sheets cannot be summarised as they are collected so that a clear and accurate picture of the things that matter, e.g. income and admissions, can be obtained almost instantly. On at least a monthly basis, a full profit and loss account and balance sheet should be prepared for full circulation and discussion.

Stage 9: revise policy or alter targets to reflect actual conditions

Rational decisions are only possible on the basis of accurate and up-to-date information. Once budget versus actual information has been analysed it provides the basis for managers to control their businesses in the most appropriate way. This may mean continuing as prescribed or altering targets and policies. Clearly there is no point in pursuing policies which are disastrous in financial terms. Equally, if an organisation is performing better than expected, then it makes sense to modify targets accordingly.

Feedback loops

Many budgeting models show feedback loops running from the end of the model back to the beginning. The integrated approach is one in which there is a continual feedback from each stage to the previous one during the budget formulation phase and the operating phase. This ensures that the objectives and their operational consequences are continually being assessed for internal consistency. This approach is also reflective of real life because the steps of the model tend not to happen in isolation. Some stages of the budget cycle happen simultaneously, typically in hectic meetings prior to the start of a new financial year. Thus it is often difficult to identify the progression from one step to the next because the budgeting cycle is normally seamless.

2 Integrated in terms of components

To give the integrated budgeting approach a framework around which to build a budget, there must be a logical sequence for putting together the financial detail of a plan. It is good management practice to integrate the strands of the master budget as they are being constructed.

The starting point for integrating components is the income or turnover budget. The importance of knowing how much money is planned to flow into a business can be summed up by one question "Is the selling price higher than the cost?" This question is still applicable to the not-for-profit sector by being modified to "Is the organisation working within the resources allocated to it?" The managerial bottom line is that whatever happens, we must work within the resources available.

To calculate the budgeted revenue requires breaking income down into its constituent parts. There is little justification, merit or logic in budgeting for unsustainable losses. Illustrated in Table 2.7 is the example used earlier in this chapter. The key variables in this case are the number of admissions and the price of the various activities.

Total Admissions	52,770	
	£s	
Entrance Fees	31,662	(60p per head)
Shoe Hire	26,385	(50p per head)
Bowling Fees	131,925	(£2.50 per head)
Cafe Income	47,493	(90p per head)
Total Income	237,465	(£4.50 per head)

Table 2.7

This kind of model is applicable to the not-for-profit sector by making the distinction between earned income and subsidy. Managers can calculate earned income as shown in Table 2.7 and then add planned subsidy to it, in order to arrive at a total income figure.

Once a clear picture of planned income has been established, the expenditure budget should be compiled. Some managers may find this approach a harrowing experience if their previous budgeting method has been to construct the expenditure budget first and then try and see how it can be financed, rather than calculating income first.

Expenditure needs to be categorised into revenue expenditure and capital expenditure. Revenue expenditure should be calculated first, as the difference between income and revenue expenditure may have a large influence on the ability to invest in fixed assets.

Each step in the construction of the integrated budget is dependent upon the last. Managers need to be continually asking themselves a question about the results being obtained. "Is this a satisfactory outcome?" If "yes", then proceed to next step. If "no", go back and revise until the outcome becomes satisfactory and then proceed.

If the outcome is acceptable after the income and revenue expenditure steps, then managers can consider the purchase of fixed assets. The only way that this can be done in an integrated manner is to analyse those items that affect the movement of cash. These can be broken down into two discrete areas, i.e. the implications for working capital (e.g. stocks, debtors and creditors) and the implications for fixed assets (e.g. buildings or equipment).

The amount of cash available will be dependent upon the time debtors take to pay our invoices, how long we take to pay our creditors and on the level of stocks (e.g. bar purchases or vending machines) that we maintain. Modelling the effect of this will tell us how much cash is available to buy fixed assets. There is little point in budgeting to spend money that we do not have as the business will inevitably fail.

Assuming that the plan remains internally consistent, the final analysis is to look at how the cash available to an organisation has changed and how this cash has been used.

Translating these common-sense requirements into a diagram of action, we can see that a third meaning of integrated budget emerges. So far we have discussed integration in terms of internal consistency and components. The third meaning is integrated in terms of financial accounting. If we translate the stages above from setting the income budget through to analysing the cash position, then the budgeting cycle can be seen to mirror closely financial accounting. This is illustrated in Table 2.8.

Budget Type	Relationship to Financial Accounting
Income Budget	Profit & Loss Account
Revenue Expenditure Budget	Profit & Loss Account
Working Capital Budget	Balance Sheet
Fixed Asset Budget	Balance Sheet
Cash Budget	Balance Sheet
Cash Movement Budget	Cash Flow Statement

Table 2.8

Budgeting methods

So far we have examined the "what" dimension of budgeting as in "what needs to be produced to make a workable financial plan?" The focus of the rest of this section will be on the actual techniques used to compile the budget. This is the "how" dimension as in "how do we or should we construct a budget?" In the same way that some budget is better than no budget, some techniques of assembling the figures that constitute a budget are better than others.

The budgeting process is fraught with problems, which are to a certain extent, inherent. So far we have assumed that decisions are made rationally, that everybody is committed to the aims of the organisation and that the budgeting process is free from political decision making. The net effect of these assumptions is that all budgeting is prepared under the conditions of what is best for the organisation. Unfortunately, these are rather ambitious foundations upon which to set about constructing a budget. Illogical management behaviour can influence the budgeting process in such a way that the budget can be sub optimised, i.e. the best possible outcome for the organisation is manipulated internally so that, in effect, a business underachieves its full potential.

To illustrate the continuum of budgeting techniques and the basic problems with budgeting, consider the two cases of the incremental budget and the zero-based budget.

1 The incremental (continuation) budget

The term "incremental budget" is a reference to a practice common to all sectors which uses last year's budget as the basis for next year's budget. The basic assumption is that the business environment conditions remain the same and that income and expenditure targets increase by the prevailing rate of inflation. As an example, consider the case of a cinema which has based the 1995 budget on what happened in 1994 and has assumed an increase in inflation of 5%. See Table 2.9.

All that has happened here is that figures have increased in line with inflation with the effect that in real terms the net profit is exactly the same in both years. There are problems with this approach to budgeting which prevent it from being recommendable.

Specific problems with incremental budgeting
(i) The retail price index (RPI) is an average estimate of how prices as a whole are moving. Differing types of income and expenditure have different rates of inflation. It would be quite possible for RPI inflation to be 5% and wage inflation 0%. Thus using a single blanket figure as an estimate for inflation is flawed.

(ii) Even if differing rates of inflation for differing budgeting headings are used, there is an implication that the objectives of the organisation have remained the same. This may not necessarily be the case and the whole of the budgeting cycle

Proposed Budget for Cinema "5% All Round Budget"				
Actual Inflation Proposed				
	1994 £s	R.P.I. %	1995 £s	
INCOME				
Ticket Revenue	150 000	5.00	157 500	
Ice Creams	35 000	5.00	36 750	
Confectionery	45 000	5.00	47 250	
Advertising	4 000	5.00	4 200	
Total Income	234 000		245 700	
EXPENDITURE				
Wages	75 000	5.00	78 750	
Premises	15 000	5.00	15 750	
Supplies	20 000	5.00	21 000	
Marketing	18 000	5.00	18 900	
Cost of Sales	67 500	5.00	70 875	
Total Expenditure	195 500		205 275	
PROFIT/(LOSS)	38 500		40 425	

Table 2.9

described above should be used, not just parts of it. Even if the same objectives are to be pursued, the decision to maintain the status quo needs to be a conscious one rather than a matter of continuity for continuity's sake.

(iii) In the cinema example above, the absolute amount of profit has increased but in real terms profitability has remained the same. The business has failed to grow, which means no new money for the upgrading of fixed assets or expansion. All organisations need to grow or to consolidate their positions. There are not many organisations that can justify planning to remain static. Incremental budgeting can be guilty of encouraging complacency.

(iv) There is a tacit assumption that management believe operating conditions will be the same. Cinema could be in a period of rapid market growth; new housing could be being built in the area; a new cinema could have opened in competition nearby – these types of variables are far more relevant than any estimate of average inflation.

General problems with incremental budgeting
At a general level in all sectors there are operational problems with incremental budgeting that illustrate its flaws even further.

(i) Those people who are responsible for setting the budget are often the same people who are required to meet the targets. It is not human nature "to make a rod for our own backs". Consequently, proposed budgets often contain a level of performance that managers know that they can meet rather than targets that they could meet. This reinforces the need for budgeting to be a participative process at all levels and the need for budgets to be approved. All levels in the chain of command should be able to identify when their staff are proposing sub optimal budgets and should request revisions to restore the balance.

(ii) There is a danger that actual versus proposed budget comparisons can replace proper performance measurement. A manager could be in a position of having underspent £200 on marketing an early riser's swimming session. On paper this looks like a positive achievement. However, if admissions are less than expected because the public have not been informed about this initiative, then clearly the saving is a false economy. It is human nature to try and make ourselves look good and we can do this by understating income and overstating expenditure in our budgets. Subsequently, when we beat our targets there is the danger that we will be thought of as doing a good job. However, if financial performance is but part of an overall appraisal system, people are far more inclined to set realistic budgets rather than ones with slack in them.

(iii) Incremental budgeting can create a situation in which unnecessary expenditure occurs out of a sense of self-preservation. This is especially the case where conditions exist such as "if you don't spend your budget by the end of the year, then you lose it", or where next year's budget is based on last year's figure plus x%. Under these conditions wasteful expenditure seems to be positively encouraged. If a manager has £500 left in a hospitality budget with a month of the financial year to go, it is possible that this money will be spent whether it needs to be or not.

(iv) By increasing budgets in an indiscriminate manner, unnecessary expenditure can be supported because it has never been challenged or justified. Staff who have systematically built in slack to their budgets will have this slack funded on an incremental basis even though it is a waste of resources. Expenditure which was intended as a one-off expense can also be perpetuated by not being queried in the budgeting cycle.

Advantages of incremental budgeting
Incremental budgeting is not all bad and there are some advantages which make it the most commonly used method for budget setting.

(i) It is an efficient way of budgeting if the initial parts of the budget cycle such as aims, policies and strategies have all remained the same. Financial periods are arbitrary timespans, and if objectives do not change within these then there is little point in trying to reinvent something which already exists.

(ii) It is relatively easy to carry out as the data upon which it is based is to hand and can be modified within the existing templates of profit and loss account, balance sheet and cash flow forecast.

(iii) It is quick to carry out and does not involve as much staff time as other budgeting methods. Consequently, it is cheaper to implement than other methods and allows staff to spend more time on the operational side of their jobs.

The opposite of the incremental budget is the zero base budget which is discussed in the next section.

2 Zero-based budgeting (ZBB)

ZBB is a budgeting method which was formulated to overcome the difficulties experienced with incremental budgeting. The starting point is not last year's figures but rather a blank piece of paper on which to start from zero. The basic assumption is that each area of expenditure needs to be justified in terms of the following questions:

- What does this expenditure aim to achieve?

- What policies will be followed to meet the aim?

- What are the benefits of this expenditure?

- What are the alternatives to this expenditure?

- What would be the effects of cutting this expenditure?

This detailed approach to every item of expenditure allows managers to rank expenditure in order of priority so that a hierarchy of prioritised expenditure is produced. If a sports centre were facing a 10% cut in its expenditure budget, the ZBB approach would be to select the top 90% of priorities rather than implement an across-the-board cut of 10%. This approach encourages a more deliberate decision-making process and its components are summarised briefly below.

(i) Determine discrete areas of expenditure within a budget, e.g. brochure printing, advertising, leaflets, posters etc.

(ii) Evaluate the benefits of each package to produce a rank order of their relative importance.

(iii) Allocate resources to the rationally identified priorities.

Example
The marketing manager of a theatre has a budget of £60,000 which has traditionally been spent on the following activities.

Bi-monthly brochures	(30,000 copies each)	24,000
Direct mail		6,000
Advertising in local press		17,000
Posters and leaflets		10,000
Office and travel expenses		3,000
Total		60,000

Income from box office sales is £150,000 and the number of tickets sold was 50,000. Recent marketing research has revealed how customers find out about the programme of events.

Season brochure	35%
Direct mail	30%
Newspaper advertising	10%
Poster or leaflets	10%
Publicity	15%
	100%

A new chief executive has been appointed at the theatre and has asked all departments to undertake a ZBB approach to their expenditure so that future options can be considered.

Possible solution

Step 1 - Identify the key expenditure packages
In this instance the main areas of expenditure can be summarised as:

- Season brochure.

- Direct mail.

- Advertising.

- Leaflets and posters.

- Publicity.

Step 2 - Evaluate the benefits of each package
(a) *Season brochure*

The season brochure generates 35% of the audiences, which yields a box office take of £150,000.

Expenditure	24,000	40% of expenditure (£60,000)
Income	52,500	35% of income (£150,000)
Balance	+28,500	surplus

(b) *Direct mail*

Direct mail generates 30% of the audiences.

Expenditure	6,000	10% of expenditure
Income	45,000	30% of income
Balance	+39,000	surplus

(c) *Advertising*

Advertising generates 10% of the audiences.

Expenditure	17,000	28% of expenditure
Income	15,000	10% of income
Balance	−2,000	deficit

(d) *Posters and leaflets*

Posters and leaflets generate 10% of the audiences.

Expenditure	10,000	17% of expenditure
Income	22,500	15% of income
Balance	+12,500	surplus

(e) *Publicity*

Publicity generates 10% of the audiences.

Expenditure	3,000	5% of expenditure
Income	15,000	10% of income
Balance	+12,000	surplus

The various packages can now be ranked into order of financial benefit to the department, as in Table 2.10.

Rank	Package	Balance	Cost	Cumulative
1st	Direct mail	+39,000	6,000	6,000
2nd	Season brochure	+28,500	24,000	30,000
3rd	Posters/leaflets	+12,500	10,000	40,000
4th	Publicity	+12,000	3,000	43,000
5th	Advertising	- 2,000	17,000	60,000
	Total	+90,000		60,000

Table 2.10

Step 3 - Allocate resources
This stage depends on what the precise objectives of the ZBB exercise are. Possibilities include: plans to reduce overall expenditure; plans to allocate exist-

ing resources more efficiently throughout an organisation; or, even, evaluating what would be the best way of allocating additional resources.

Scenario 1: reduce expenditure by £12,000 (20%)
By examining the hierarchy of benefits, it is clear that advertising expenditure is not particularly effective relative to the other methods. This would be the first area in which cuts would be made. If £17,000 worth of advertising expenditure leads to £15,000 worth of income, we can estimate that by cutting expenditure to £5,000, the revised income would be £4,412. This can now be put into the overall model to see the final result, as in Table 2.11.

	Cost	Income	Balance
Direct mail	6,000	45,000	+39,000
Season brochure	24,000	52,500	+28,500
Posters/leaflets	10,000	22,500	+12,500
Publicity	3,000	15,000	+12,000
Advertising	5,000	4,412	-588
Totals	48,000	139,412	+91,412

Table 2.11

In this case, it has been possible to reduce expenditure and increase income in a rational manner which is more favourable to a 20% cut across the board which would have an entirely different effect. It is assumed that income and costs maintain the relationships identified by the marketing research. See Table 2.12.

	Cost (-20%)	Income (-20%)	Balance
Direct mail	4,800	36,000	+31,200
Season brochure	19,200	42,000	+22,800
Posters/leaflets	8,000	18,000	+10,000
Publicity	2,400	12,000	+9,600
Advertising	13,600	12,000	1,600
Totals	48,000	120,000	+72,000

Table 2.12

The difference of £19,412 between the balance of +£91,412 and +£72,000 respectively is a powerful argument to support the ZBB approach rather than an across the board approach.

Scenario 2: allocating additional resources
It is not really possible to predict what would happen in this case without addi-

tional information. However, the basic principle is clear, i.e. rather than increasing all expenditure packages by a set percentage, a rational evaluation is necessary. In this case it would seem that direct mail would be the most sensible package to devote any extra funds to.

General issues with Zero-Based Budgeting

Used sensibly, ZBB has much to commend it in terms of being able to allocate resources in a systematic manner. This is based on the assumption that all staff prioritise the best interests of an organisation and its strategic aims. However, implementing and using ZBB does have its difficulties.

(i) ZBB cannot be conducted in isolation from other basic management functions. In the worked example above, the ZBB approach was based on management information identified by marketing research. Thus, to be able to make useful ZBB decisions it is necessary to also have a performance measurement system in place.

(ii) The time and resources needed to implement ZBB can be wasteful, particularly if there has been no change of policy or operating procedures. Rather than use ZBB all of the time, it may be an effective compromise to use it as part of a three- or five-yearly review cycle. For example, a leisure centre operating under a CCT contract would be advised to use ZBB in making the initial tender but not necessarily for the duration of the contract. When the contract was due for renewal in, say, four years, it would make sense to use ZBB again.

(iii) Managers' perceptions of ZBB are usually negative, particularly if they are not familiar with it. Often this is on the basis of prior experience where ZBB has been inflicted from above, with little thought and unrealistic timetables. Another example of inappropriate use of ZBB is senior management trying to solve political problems with a rational management technique. However, research does indicate that those managers who have actually used ZBB over a period of years tend to realise its benefits and are more positive about it than non-users.

Summary

The focus of this chapter has been to illustrate the steps that are needed to put together a budget and the methods that are used to do this in practice. The key learning points have been as follows:

(i) To realise how financial statements relate to one another and to understand the significance of the expanded profit and loss account, balance sheet and cash flow statement.

(ii) To understand the importance of "when" money is planned to be spent as well as "how much" is planned to be spent.

(iii) To appreciate the need to simulate the financial consequences of given events occuring in the future.

(iv) To be aware of the range of information required to make rational decisions.

(v) To understand the various budgeting techniques that are available to managers and to know the suitability of their application in given circumstances.

Chapter 3 develops these ideas by illustrating the processes that should be used when implementing good practice in budgeting.

Review and management applications
Having read this chapter you should now be in the position to apply some of the following questions to your own organisation.

(1) Do you produce budgeted profit and loss accounts, balance sheets and cash flow statements?

(2) What technique do you typically use to compile the budget for next year?

(3) Would your organisation gain from adopting the zero-based budgeting approach?

(4) Do you have an ongoing strategic planning process, and are financial statements an integral part of it?

(5) Is the integrated budget approach an academic pipedream or a model of good practice?

Further reading

Riddle, G. (1983) *Stage One Cost Accounting*, Northwick Publishers, Worcester.

Cook, P. et al (1992) *Local Authority Budget Guide*, Longman, London.

Gratton, C. and Taylor, P. (1985) *Sport and Recreation an Economic Analysis*, E. & F.N. Spon, London.

Naylor, D. (1992) *Financial Decision Making in Leisure and Recreation Management*, Ravenswood Publications Ltd, London.

Chapter 3
Information for management control

Objectives

The objective of this chapter is to illustrate how financial information should be presented in order to be meaningful. It is one thing to participate in the monitoring and review process, it is another thing for this process to be worthwhile. Using the ideas presented in this chapter, managers will have an insight into the following areas of management control:

(i) To show precisely what information is required and how it should be presented in a good budgeting and reporting system.

(ii) To demonstrate how the analysis of budgetary variances should be used to provide maximum meaningful information.

(iii) To introduce management issues in budgeting such as budgetary virements and cost centring.

1 Information requirements

The major feature about analysing financial information is the reporting of what has actually happened compared with what was planned to happen. This provides the basis for identifying those areas where a business is performing well or where it is experiencing difficulties. Once these variances have been identified, it then becomes possible to take whatever remedial action is required to handle any situation rationally.

Example
If a leisure pool is losing money when it was set up to make a profit, then it will be necessary for the owners to take corrective action by controlling their business. This requires the information upon which a management decision is made to be accurate and available quickly.

Example
If an aerobics session is proving so popular that customers are being turned away, then costings need to be done to investigate either putting on additional sessions or alternatively increasing the price. The only way in which these decisions can be made sensibly is if the supporting financial information is available.

The remainder of this section illustrates the ways in which budgetary data should be presented in order to provide managers with an accurate and comprehensive view of their organisation's financial performance.

The starting point

In practice, the most commonly used financial statement is the profit and loss account. It illustrates how an organisation's net worth (capital or reserves) has changed over a given period of time. If the profit and loss account is performing badly, then this will be reflected in the balance sheet. The conventional manner of presenting financial statements is in the predetermined order of: profit and loss account, balance sheet and cash flow statement. You can prove this for yourself by examining any set of published accounts.

The profit and loss account needs to be broken down into discrete units, such as months, so that measurement of *actual* performance versus *budgeted* performance can be measured. This needs to happen in two formats: firstly, *actual* versus *budget* for the month in question; and, secondly, *actual* versus *budget* on a cumulative basis, i.e. since the start of the financial year.

Example
Consider the case of a leisure centre which has both wet and dry facilities. A simplified monthly profit and loss account reflecting the financial objective of breaking even at the end of the year is presented below. What financial information does the manager need to assess the performance of the centre at the end of May?

INCOME	April	May	June	July	Aug.	Sept.	Oct.	Nov.	Dec.	Jan.	Feb.	March	Total
Swimming	9000	8000	6000	5000	6000	7000	9000	8000	9000	7000	8000	6000	88000
Hall hire	4050	3600	2700	2250	2700	3150	4050	3600	4050	3150	3600	2700	39600
Multi-gym	2250	2000	1500	1250	1500	1750	2250	2000	2250	1750	2000	1500	22000
Health suite	1350	1200	900	750	900	1050	1350	1200	1350	1050	1200	900	13200
Total	16650	14800	11100	9250	11100	12950	16650	14800	16650	12950	14800	11100	162800
Cumulative	16650	31450	42550	51800	62900	75850	92500	107300	123950	136900	151700	162800	
EXPENDITURE													
Salaries	3500	3500	3500	3500	3500	3500	3500	3500	3500	3500	3500	3500	42000
Wages	3330	2960	2220	1850	2220	2590	3330	2960	3330	2590	2960	2220	32560
Building	6000	2500	3000	6000	1000	600	2000	3000	1250	4000	2000	1500	32850
Services	2498	2220	1665	1388	1665	1943	2498	2220	2498	1943	2220	1665	24420
Office	1225	1225	1225	1225	1225	1225	1225	1225	1225	1225	1225	1225	14700
Marketing	1665	1480	1110	925	1110	1295	1665	1480	1665	1295	1480	1100	16270
Total	18218	13885	12720	14888	10720	11153	14218	14385	13468	14553	13385	11210	162800
Cumulative	18218	32103	44823	59710	70430	81583	95800	110185	123653	138205	151590	162800	
BALANCE	-1568	915	-1620	-5638	380	1798	2433	415	3183	-1603	1415	-110	0
Cumulative	-1568	-653	-2273	-7910	-7530	-5733	-3300	-2885	298	-1305	110	0	

Figure 3.1   Budgeted monthly profit & loss account, leisure centre budget

As a result of the efficiency of the finance officer, the financial performance for the month of April has been prepared previously and is summarised in Figure 3.2.

	Actual	Incurred	Total	Budget	Variance	U/F
INCOME						
Swimming	9 100		9 100	9 000	100	F
Hall hire	4 025		4 025	4 050	−25	U
Multi-gym	2 375		2 375	2 250	125	F
Health suite	1 400		1 400	1 350	50	F
Total	16 900	0	16 900	16 650	250	F
EXPENDITURE						
Salaries	3 475		3 475	3 500	−25	F
Wages	3 350		3 350	3 330	20	U
Building	6 125		6 125	6 000	125	U
Services	2 300	200	2 500	2 498	3	U
Office	1 150		1 150	1 225	−75	F
Marketing	1 800		1 800	1 665	135	U
Total	18 200	200	18 400	18 218	183	U
BALANCE	−1 300	−200	−1 500	−1 568	68	F

Figure 3.2   Leisure centre budget financial report for April

Since the manager has already seen the performance of April, the key information deficiency is May's trading. This is shown in Figure 3.3, as a month-only budget report.

	Actual	Incurred	Total	Budget	Variance	U/F	Note
INCOME							
Swimming	8 200		8 200	8 000	200	F	1
Hall hire	3 200		3 200	3 600	−400	U	2
Multi-gym	2 300		2 300	2 000	300	F	3
Health suite	1 450		1 450	1 200	250	F	3
Total	15 150	0	15 150	14 800	350	F	
EXPENDITURE							
Salaries	3 500		3 500	3 500	0	(-)	
Wages	3 200		3 200	2 960	240	U	4
Building	1 200	1 100	2 300	2 500	−200	F	5
Services	2 300		2 300	2 220	80	U	
Office	1 150		1 150	1 225	−75	F	
Marketing	1 500		1 500	1 480	20	U	
Total	12 850	1 100	13 950	13 885	65	U	
BALANCE	2 300	−1 100	1 200	915	285	F	

Figure 3.3   Leisure centre budget financial report for May

Note 1 – Swimming
The favourable variance of £200 can be explained by attracting more admissions for the Saturday afternoon inflatable sessions than originally planned.

Note 2 - Hall hire
The unfavourable variance of £400 is accounted for by the last minute cancellation of a trade exhibition that had been booked in. This represents an actual loss in hire fees.

Note 3 – Multi-gym and health suite
The combined favourable variance of £550 on these two accounts is explained by the success of a direct marketing campaign to introduce new members. The campaign has exceeded the budgeted target by 20 members.

Note 4 – Wages
The overspend of £240 on wages is explained by needing additional staff time to induct new members to the multi-gym and health suite. Additional lifeguards have also been used to cope with the increased numbers of swimmers using the pool.

Note 5 – Building
The incurred figure of £1,100 is for budgeted routine maintenance work. This work has been carried out to our satisfaction but the suppliers have not yet submitted their invoices. The overall underspend of £200 on building costs is the result of an energy saving campaign that has resulted in this actual saving.

Meaningful information

What are the features about this *actual* versus *budget* comparison that make it meaningful? There are two main answers to this question: firstly, the report provides quantitative information on performance; and, secondly, the notes provide a qualitative dimension to the report which explains the significance of the figures.

The use of actual figures
When compiling a budget report, it is essential that the figures which are used reconcile to whatever accounting system is being used. There is nothing to be gained (except errors) by running two or more systems in parallel. Actual figures mean those which have been entered into the accounting system and which are supported by documentary evidence, such as time sheets, invoices or till rolls.

The use of incurred figures
It is often the case that suppliers do not submit their invoices in time to be included as actual figures in the accounts. By not allowing for this we are often in danger of understating our expenditure. We can allow for this by the introduction of an "incurred" or "committed" column which gives a more realistic picture of the financial events that have taken place. The advantages of an incurred column are: firstly, it allows the presentation of actual figures as they appear in the accounts; and, secondly, it also allows for management adjustments to be made.

Comparison with budget figures
The whole point about budgeting is to compare what has actually happened to what was planned to happen. By having the total and the budget columns next to one another, it is possible to calculate the variance between the two. Bearing in mind that accounts are often presented to non-finance people, good practice means making things simple for the reader. Using the format above, even the untrained eye can see at a glance how the figures have been derived.

Favourable or unfavourable?
Most people are not interested in variances *per se* but rather "is this good or bad?" There are no uniformly adopted methods of reporting variances, i.e. actual minus budget is used equally as much as budget minus actual. Thus the onus is very

much on the budget report writer to make the variances easy to understand. The simple convention of "F" (favourable) for extra income or reduced expenditure and "U" (unfavourable) for reduced income or increased expenditure is a helpful reporting device.

Qualitative explanations
It is one thing to calculate variances in actual versus budget comparisons but, as above, what readers are really interested in is the underlying significance of the figures. Often it is helpful to explain variances with a note so that readers are not misled or even forced to invent their own interpretations.

The bottom line of May's budget report is that despite various fluctuations in some of the budget versus actual comparisons, the centre is £285 better off than it had planned to be. This is useful information in the context of one month in isolation but also needs to be considered in the cumulative context since the beginning of the financial year.

Cumulative budget report
Using the individual monthly reports from Figures 3.2 and 3.3, it is now possible to construct a cumulative budget for the two months April and May. All that is happening is that the corresponding columns are being added together to give an overall total for the year so far. In addition to the basic monthly figures, it is also possible to build in other useful information that will provide managers with a more informative overview of performance to date. This is shown in Figure 3.4.

	Actual	Incurred	Total	Budget	Variance	U/F	Note	Budget Remaining	Year End Forecast
INCOME									
Swimming	17 300*		17 300	17 000	300	F	1	71 000	91 500
Hall hire	7 225		7 225	7 650	−425	U	2	31 950	38 500
Multi-gym	4 675		4 675	4 250	425	F	3	17 750	24 000
Health suite	2 850		2 850	2 550	300	F	3	10 650	15 000
Total	32 050	0	32 050	31 450	600	F		131 350	169 000

*17 300 = x (April actual) plus y (May actual)

	Actual	Incurred	Total	Budget	Variance	U/F	Note	Budget Remaining	Year End Forecast
EXPENDITURE									
Salaries	6 975		6 975	7 000	−25	F		35 000	43 000
Wages	6 550		6 550	6 290	260	U	4	26 270	35 000
Building	7 325	1 100	8 425	8 500	−75	F		24 350	31 500
Services	4 600	200	4 800	4 718	83	U		19 703	24 500
Office	2 300		2 300	2 450	−150	F	5	12 250	14 700
Marketing	3 300		3 300	3 145	155	U		13 125	16 200
Total	31 050	1 300	32 350	32 103	248	U		130 698	164 900
BALANCE	1 000	−1 300	−300	−653	353	F	6	653	4 100

Figure 3.4 Leisure centre budget, cumulative financial report for April and May

As well as the positive features for the May report, the cumulative budget has some useful additional features that provide managers with even more information with which to control the business.

The budget remaining column

This tells managers what has been planned to happen for the rest of the year (in this case another 10 months). In the case of income, it is a measure of how much more turnover is required, and in the case of expenditure it tells how much money is left to spend in any given budget. The net result of this column is that it sets targets for those in control of budgets. The budget remaining data is particularly valuable the further you get into a financial year. It enables managers to set upper limits on expenditure and to have clear targets for income. The advantage of this column is that it can identify areas of potential underperformance well in advance of the event occurring. This is precisely the kind of information that is required for effective control. Making the decisions is easy if you have accurate supporting information.

The year end forecast

A forecast is defined as a prediction of what might occur in a given situation. This contrasts with a budget which is a detailed financial plan that an organisation is trying to achieve. In this case, the year end forecast is a statement such as "given our performance so far over two months, what will be result at the year end if we maintain current performance?" The year end forecast provides a link between actual performance and budgeted performance which permits further control. If the projected forecast is negative, it provides managers with sufficient time to take remedial action rather than wait for the events to happen. If, as in this case, the year end forecast is positive, then it encourages managers to pursue the policies that are causing this success.

Clarity

In this context, clarity means that the performance of the organisation can be seen at a glance. To the end of May a loss of £653 was planned for and in reality the figure achieved was a loss of only £300. For those people who wish to have further details, these are contained in the accompanying set of notes. There is a trade-off between providing every single piece of information and being concise. By being too comprehensive there is the danger that the essentials become lost in a sea of trivia, and by being too concise managers run the risk of devaluing the reporting statements. The pragmatic compromise is to report the essential facts but to have supporting information available if it is required.

Some readers may feel that the level of detail required in the presentation of a budget report is such that they would have to spend all of their time playing with numbers. This is not necessarily the case. One of the most important devices in a manager's financial skills portfolio is the ability to use a computer spreadsheet. Section 5 will illustrate how some of the financial tables in this manual have been produced by the use of spreadsheets.

In the same way that the profit and loss account has been analysed as above, a suitably adapted format can be used to monitor actual versus budget for the balance sheet and the cash flow position.

2 Management applications of incurred expenditure

The major problem with reporting financial information is that in the rush to provide management accounts quickly, expenditure is frequently understated. This, in effect, devalues the information provided by failing to observe the essential requirement of accuracy. The pragmatic solution to this problem lies in a device known as the "expenditure control sheet".

Expenditure control sheet

The theory behind the expenditure control sheet is simple: those people who have the authority to spend money also have a responsibility to record their expenditure. If an expenditure control sheet is filled in for every month or other financial period, then two vital pieces of information become available: firstly, those expenses which have been processed will agree with the balance in the financial accounts; and, secondly, those invoices which have not been processed can be entered accurately as incurred expenditure. The net result is that both actual and incurred expenditure will now reconcile with their constituent parts.

To see this system in practice, a worked example is shown below. Figure 3.5 shows one line (hospitality expenses) from the profit and loss account. Figure 3.6 shows how, in a well-run system, actual and incurred expenditure reconcile with the budget controller's own records.

EXPENDITURE	Actual	Incurred	Total	Budget	Variance	U/F
Hospitality	342	152	494	500	6	F

Figure 3.5   Leisure centre budget, financial report for June

One of the benefits of expenditure control sheets is that when filled out correctly, they provide managers with a direct link between their own expenditure and the final accounts. Theoretically, actual expenditure, as stated in the accounts, should equal the total of expenditure for which vouchers have been received by the accounts department. Also, any incurred figure in the accounts should equal the sum of any expenditure for which vouchers have not been received. Often budget controllers will make statements at meetings such as "those figures are wrong", which is negative and potentially disruptive. If the same budget controllers maintain expenditure control sheets, if they disagree with a set of figures, they are in a position to offer an explanation. Negative remarks can now give way to a positive alternative, for example, "my figures do not agree with yours, can we have a meeting to see where the discrepancy is?"

Once this sort of system is in place, it is often amazing to see the improvement in the working relationship between budget controllers and accounts staff. The use of expenditure control sheets is neither difficult nor technical. It relies on a commitment from all staff who spend money to account for their transactions in a systematic manner and to liaise with the finance department where necessary.

```
Budget Heading:                  Expenses - Centre Manager

Budget Code   : H104

Details of Expenditure:

                              Order Number/        Net      Voucher
       Date      Supplier     Purchase Type      Amount     Recorded

        2/6      Centre cafe    Petty cash         24.58       Yes
        8/6      Queen's hotel  Order No. 625     115.34       No
       10/6      Bar            Petty cash         12.92       Yes
       14/6      Going Places   Order No. 628     225.50       Yes
       20/6      SS Taxis       Standing order     22.00       Yes
       24/6      Jo Lasagnes    Direct debit       50.00       Yes
       28/6      Bar            Recharge voucher    7.00       Yes
       30/6      Wilford Arms   Order No. 630      36.66       No

                                 Total =          494.00


Total for vouchers recorded =    342.00 (balances to accounts)

Total for vouchers incurred =    152.00 (show as incurred)

        8/6      Queen's hotel   Order No. 625    115.34       No
       30/6      Wilford Arms    Order No. 630     36.66       No

                                 Total incurred =  152.00

Overall total =                  494.00 (balances to total above)
```

Figure 3.6   Expenditure control sheet financial period: June 1994

3 The analysis of variances

No matter how hard managers try, it is highly unlikely that actual income and expenditure will match planned income and expenditure exactly. In practice it is probable that there will be a variance on every single actual versus budget comparison. Some variances will be insignificant and require no detailed investigation; others will require considerable investigation and expansion.

There is little to be gained by reporting on every single budget variance. Clarity means concentrating on the essential figures and ignoring trivia. In recognition of this, certain conventions are adopted to make the reporting of variances meaningful. The major types of variances split into two discrete categories, i.e. timing variances and actual variances.

Timing variance

A timing variance occurs when what is planned to happen and what actually happens do not coincide in the same financial period. These variances are also known as "cash flow variances". This is an incorrect description because accounts are prepared on an accruals basis rather than a cash basis.

Example

In local authorities, wages are linked to a scale on which staff receive a seniority rise in April and a cost of living rise in July. When preparing next year's budget, managers need to estimate the cost of living rise to construct their budgets. A further complication is that often the actual cost of living rise is not settled between management and unions until after July.

The subsequent effects on the budget are twofold: firstly, during the period in which the cost of living rise is unsettled, actual expenditure is understated; and, secondly, when the pay rise is finally settled, expenditure is overstated because of the back pay which is paid to staff.

The overall effect of timing variances is not normally significant because they cancel each other out over time. It is sufficient to report in the notes to a set of accounts that a variance is caused by a timing difference rather than an actual overspend or underspend.

Minimising timing variances

The effects of timing variances on budget reporting can be minimised in the construction of the budget by the use of two reporting devices:

(i) *The use of incurred expenditure.* In the local authorities' wages example above, variances could be minimised by showing actual expenditure and an estimate of incurred expenditure. The incurred expenditure can be estimated by calculating the difference between what was planned to happen (budget) and what has happened (actual).

Example

Unadjusted budget report for wages account:

Expenditure	Actual	Incurred	Total	Budget	Variance	Note
Wages	11 500	0	11 500	12 250	750 (F)	

Adjusted budget report for wages account:

Expenditure	Actual	Incurred	Total	Budget	Variance	Note
Wages	11500	750	12250	12250	0	1

Note 1: The incurred figure of £750 represents the budgeted cost of living rise for the month. This has not yet been paid to staff because management and unions have not formally settled the current pay round. The incurred sum will be paid to staff as back pay pending formal agreement of the pay settlement.

The adjusted report and accompanying note is more helpful to management as the additional qualitative information clarifies any possible misunderstanding. The worst thing that could happen here would be for the apparent saving to be vired (transferred) into another account because managers thought that they had made a saving! The basic attention to detail shown above, will prevent this sort of disaster from happening.

(ii) *Preparing accounts on a real life basis.* The only way to make budget versus actual comparison meaningful, is if the budget is close to reality. In practice this means preparing a budget in a way that reflects how things are planned to happen.

Example

Electricity charges are not usually the same throughout the year for leisure venues. Typically, we use less during the summer and more during the winter. Equally, electricity companies charge more for their electricity during the winter than the summer. Therefore, when putting together a budget, managers should always plan for the final budget to be as close to reality as possible.

Method 1: Equal amounts per month
Six-monthly budget

Expenditure	Jan	Feb	March	April	May	June	July	Total
Electricity	2 000	2 000	2 000	2 000	2 000	2 000	2 000	14 000

Method 2: When the bill arrives
Six-monthly budget

Expenditure	Jan	Feb	March	April	May	June	July	Total
Electricity	3 000	3 000	3 000	2 500	1 000	750	750	14 000

Imagine that at the end of March the cumulative expenditure on electricity was £9,200. What would the budget report of each method look like? There are two methods for producing an adjusted budget report for the electricity account.

Method 1

Expenditure	Actual	Incurred	Total	Budget	Variance	Note
Electricity	9 200	0	9 200	6 000	–3 200 (U)	1

Note 1: The unfavourable variance of £3,200 is explained by two factors: firstly, an inability to budget properly amounting to £3,000; and, secondly, an actual over-spend of £200.

Method 2

Expenditure	Actual	Incurred	Total	Budget	Variance	Note
Electricity	9 200	0	9 200	9 000	–200 (U)	1

Note 1: The unfavourable variance of £200 is an actual overspend. Action in the form of an energy saving campaign is now being taken to recover this loss.

Clearly method 2 is more useful to management as it has isolated the £200 overspend which is the important issue in this example. Method 1 requires an explanation about the poor budgeting and the overspend. Good budget reporting means concentrating only on the business essentials and not becoming bogged down in trivia or timing differences.

Actual variance

An actual variance occurs when an unplanned overspend or an underspend takes place. This concept is illustrated in the following two examples.

Example 1: actual overspend

A leisure centre has budgeted for a cost of living rise of 3% for its staff. Good union negotiators have managed to persuade management to settle for 5%. What are the effects on the budget?

Expenditure	Actual	Incurred	Total	Budget	Variance	Note
Wages	10 500	0	10 500	10 300	−200 (U)	1

Note 1: The unfavourable variance of £200 has been caused by a higher than planned for wages settlement. With eight months of the financial year left, the forecast over-spend on this account will be £1,600 unless appropriate control is exercised.

Example 2: actual underspend

A hotel manager has introduced an itemised telephone billing system to prevent staff from making personal calls.

Expenditure	Actual	Incurred	Total	Budget	Variance	Note
Telephone	575	0	575	700	+125 (F)	1

Note 1: The under-spend of £125 is an actual saving created by the use of an itemised telephone billing option. This has resulted in a reduction in unauthorised use of the hotel's telephone system. It is anticipated that this initiative will save £500 during the course of the year.

The key difference between timing and actual variances is that actual variances have management implications that may or may not need to be acted upon. Timing variances, by contrast, will eventually cancel themselves out. Thus in the actual overspend example above, if management do not control the business, then they will be £1,600 adrift of where they planned to be on the wages account.

People who read budget reports are often not specialists in financial management. Therefore, they do not want to read reams of paper to discover that a hotel is £50 ahead of budget after six months. To deliver an appropriate budget report requires "reporting by exception" rather than reporting all variances. In practice this means that budgets should be prepared in a methodical way so as to minimise the possibility of timing variances. When actual variances occur, they can be readily identified as such. This enables managers to forecast the implications of these actual variances, to implement appropriate control where necessary and to concentrate solely on the important issues when making financial reports.

4 Budgetary virements

The term "virement" is used in budgetary terms to describe the transfer of income or expenditure from one budget account to another. There are two types of budgetary virements: management virements and policy virements. A management virement is a reallocation of income or expenditure within a budget which results in no net change to the planned outcome. A policy virement is a reallocation of income or expenditure which does have an effect to the planned outcome. To understand what is meant by these types of virement in practice, consider the following two examples.

Example 1: management virements

A sports centre manager has a supplies and services budget as indicated below. There is a one week residential management course which he would like to attend costing £950.

Supplies and services	Amount
Travel	500
Hospitality	1 200
Stationery	2 000
Telephone	650
Professional fees	3 250
Training and development	250
Total	7 850

Clearly, attending the course is not feasible within the existing training budget of £250. However, it could become possible by reallocating funds from elsewhere. In this case, the manager decides that by being careful with his hospitality he can save £400, and by re-negotiating with the accountants he can save an additional £300. Under these circumstances the virement would appear as demonstrated below.

Supplies and services	Original Budget	Virement	Revised Budget
Travel	500	0	500
Hospitality	1 200	−400	800
Stationery	2 000	0	2 000
Telephone	650	0	650
Professional fees	3 250	−300	2 950
Training and development	250	+700	950
Total	7 850	0	7 850

The point of note here is that no change occurs to the absolute amount of budget for supplies and services. What has happened is merely a limited reallocation of resources within the original budget.

Example 2: policy virements

The manager of a private health club has tabled a marketing campaign to his board of directors for their approval. The bottom line of the campaign is that by spending £2,000 on target marketing at least 50 new members each paying £300 per year will join the club. The original budget for the club is illustrated below.

Income	Amount
Membership (300 @ £300)	90 000
Casual Usage	20 000
Catering and Bar	45 000
Other Income	7 000
Total	162 000
Expenditure	
Purchases	22 000
Wages	42 000
Premises	14 000
Supplies	9 500
Marketing	3 500
Other Expenses	11 000
Total	102 000
Net Profit	60 000

The proposed marketing campaign seems to make good sense and it can be modelled by examining the effects of spending the additional £2,000. For the sake of simplicity, it will be assumed that no other income or cost budgets will be affected by the proposal.

Income	Original Budget	Virement	Revised Budget
Membership (300 @ £300)	90 000	+15 000	105 000
Casual Usage	20 000	0	20 000
Catering and Bar	45 000	0	45 000
Other Income	7 000	0	7 000
Total	162 000	+15 000	177 000
Expenditure			
Purchases	22 000	0	22 000
Wages	42 000	0	42 000
Premises	14 000	0	14 000
Supplies	9 500	0	9 500
Marketing	3 500	+2 000	5 500
Other Expenses	11 000	0	11 000
Total	102 000	+2 000	104 000
Net Profit	60 000	+13 000	73 000

Assuming that this marketing proposition is accepted, then it can be seen how a policy decision has been taken which affects the planned outcome of the private health club.

Management and policy virements are often the practical outcome of an ongoing policy of monitoring and review. Budgets need to be responsive to their environments. Using budget virements is a useful device to respond to changes as they occur. For example, if a business is making more money than expected, then the budgeted net profit can be increased accordingly. Equally, if a business is experiencing difficulties, cut-backs can be implemented to enable income and expenditure to maintain a satisfactory balance.

Problems with budgetary virements

On the surface, budget virements seem to be the ideal device to keep actual and budgeted performance reasonably close to each other. Used within the spirit of good management practice, virements have an important role to play in the continuous review and control phases of the budget cycle. However, virements are not without their difficulties. Three main problems can be identified:

(i) Virements may not be permitted in an organisation. This is particularly true of the public sector. As an example, a conscientious manager may save £5,000 on wages and ask for the money to be spent on a computer. If this proposal is outside of an authority's standing orders or the committee refuse to approve it, then, no matter how obvious the logic, the proposal will not be accepted. The solution to this problem is simple – managers need to know the parameters they are operating within and observe them. Those people who make the rules need to be explicit and consistent.

(ii) Virements can mask inefficiency in budgetary control. Virements have been misused by unscrupulous managers transferring funds from an underspend in one area to conceal an overspend in another. This has little to do with rational management control and a lot to do with financial "window dressing", i.e. making things appear different compared with reality. The solution to this problem is that all virements should be approved before they are implemented and be presented in the format illustrated above (p 50). Additionally, qualitative information should be provided to explain the purpose of any virement.

(iii) Virements can be used cynically. There is evidence of managers securing funds for projects which have funding available and then transferring the money to other budgets. This too has little to do with rational management. The solution to this problem is the use of zero-based budgeting so that the opportunities for building in "slush funds" are minimised.

5 Cost centre management

The use of cost centres is a device which brings clarity to a set of financial statements by dividing the activities of an organisation into clearly defined and separately accountable units.

As an example, a sports centre may have a swimming pool, sports hall and catering/bar facilities. It is in the interests of management at all levels to see how each area of a business or cost centre has performed in isolation. This avoids the case of good performance in one area masking poor performance in another. Also, cost centring enables management to see to what extent objectives are being met in financial terms. It is unlikely that a local authority would be pleased to see that the users of sunbeds were being subsidised by profits from swimming lessons. By using cost centres it is possible to identify those areas of a business which are performing to plan and those which are not.

What is a cost centre?

Cost centring does not happen by mistake, it is a carefully thought out process that will only work under given conditions which are discussed below.

(i) Every aspect of a business that is being cost centred must be clearly defined, e.g. the "wet" side of a sports centre or the bar and catering areas of a theatre. One of the most common problems of cost centring is an inability or unwillingness to define and allocate the relevant costs accordingly.

(ii) The cost centre must have a manager or supervisor nominally in charge of it. This person should have responsibility for the operational and financial performance of their cost centre. The key point about cost centring is that it allocates unequivocal financial accountability to the person responsible for it. This contrasts favourably with the situation in which managers can often avoid individual accountability by hiding behind the performance of an organisation as a whole.

(iii) The customers of a cost centre should be readily identifiable as such. In practical terms this means that it should be possible to identify how much income should be allocated to a cost centre. In a bar, for example, it is likely that there will be a till behind the bar and thus income can be recorded directly. Similarly, at reception it must be possible to identify types of users, e.g. swimmers, sports hall users etc. This can be achieved by the use of different prices for each activity, a PLU (price look up) till or a computerised booking system.

(iv) In accounting terms, a cost centre must be able to be viewed in isolation from the rest of the organisation. This is the only way in which performance can be monitored effectively. In practice this means that the budget must be divided in such a way that all incomes and costs can be allocated to a cost centre accurately.

(v) There must be an organisation-wide commitment to make cost centring work and a willingness to experiment in the early stages whilst the allocation of indirect costs can be assessed accurately.

Example
Imagine that the final accounts of a sports centre are as displayed below. It can be seen that the required surplus of £5 000 has been achieved. However, it is not possible to identify how each of the three areas have performed in isolation.

INCOME	Actual	Budget	Variance	(U/F)
Swimming Pool	120 000	140 000	−20 000	U
Sports Hall	70 000	75 000	−5 000	U
Bar & Catering	115 000	85 000	30 000	F
Total	305 000	300 000	5 000	F
EXPENDITURE				
Wages & Salaries	128 000	125 000	3 000	U
Bar & Catering Purchases	54 000	40 000	14 000	U
Building Costs	63 000	65 000	−2 000	F
Supplies & Services	41 000	42 000	−1 000	F
Marketing	9 000	12 000	−3 000	F
Other Expenses	5 000	11 000	−6 000	F
Total	300 000	295 000	5 000	U
BALANCE	5 000	5 000	0	–

Cost centring requires managers to identify the costs which are specific to a given cost centre and to allocate them accordingly. For this example, assume that costs are split in the following proportions.

Wages and salaries:

Bar & Catering   = 20% of bar and catering turnover
                 = 20% of 85 000
                 = £17 000

Swimming Pool   = 65% of remaining staff budget
                = 65% of (125 000–17 000)
                = £70 200

Sports Hall   = 35% of remaining staff budget
                = 35% of (125 000–17 000)
                = £37 800

Total   = £125 000

Bar and catering purchases (cost of sales):

Purchases   = 47% of sales
                = 47% of 85 000
                = £40 000

Building costs:

	Percent	Total Budget	Cost Centre Budget
Swimming Pool	58%	65 000	38 000
Sports Hall	26%	65 000	17 000
Bar & Catering	16%	65 000	10 000
Totals	100%		65 000

Supplies and services:

	Percent	Total Budget	Cost Centre Budget
Swimming Pool	43%	42 000	18 000
Sports Hall	40%	42 000	17 000
Bar & Catering	17%	42 000	7 000
Totals	100%		42 000

Marketing:

	Percent	Total Budget	Cost Centre Budget
Swimming Pool	33%	12 000	4 000
Sports Hall	50%	12 000	6 000
Bar & Catering	17%	12 000	2 000
Totals	100%		12 000

Other expenses:

	Percent	Total Budget	Cost Centre Budget
Swimming Pool	64%	11 000	7 000
Sports Hall	18%	11 000	2 000
Bar & Catering	18%	11 000	2 000
Totals	100%		11 000

These figures can now be used to construct a budget against which to compare the performance of the three cost centres in isolation. For simplicity, imaginary actual figures have been used to illustrate how a cost centred budget might appear for internal management purposes. See Figure 3.7.

	Actual	Budget	Variance	(U/F)
INCOME				
Swimming Pool	120 000	140 000	–20 000	U
EXPENDITURE				
Wages & Salaries	–63 000	–70 200	7 200	F
Building Costs	–37 000	–38 000	1 000	F
Supplies & Services	–16 000	–18 000	2 000	F
Marketing	–2 000	–4 000	2 000	F
Other Expenses	–4 000	–7 000	3 000	F
Sub Total	–122 000	–137 200	15 200	F
PROFIT/LOSS	–2 000	2 800	–4 800	U
INCOME				
Sports Hall	70 000	75 000	–5 000	U
EXPENDITURE				
Wages & Salaries	–35 000	–37 800	2 800	F
Building Costs	–14 000	–17 000	3 000	F
Supplies & Services	–13 000	–17 000	4 000	F
Marketing	–6 000	–6 000	0	F
Other Expenses	–500	–2 000	1 500	F
Sub Total	–68 500	–79 800	11 300	F
PROFIT/LOSS	1 500	-4 800	6 300	F
INCOME				
Bar & Catering	115 000	85 000	30 000	F
Bar & Catering Purchases	–54 000	–40 000	–14 000	U
GROSS PROFIT	61 000	45 000	16 000	F
EXPENDITURE				
Wages & Salaries	–30 000	–17 000	–13 000	U
Building Costs	–12 000	–10 000	–2 000	U
Supplies & Services	–12 000	–7 000	–5 000	F
Marketing	–1 000	–2 000	1 000	F
Other Expenses	–500	–2 000	1 500	F
Sub Total	–55 500	38 000	–17 500	U
PROFIT/LOSS	5 500	7 000	–1 500	U
SUMMARY				
Total Income	305 000	300 000	5 000	F
Total Expenditure	300 000	295 000	–5 000	U
BALANCE	5 000	5 000	0	-

Figure 3.7   Cost-centred budget for internal management use

The points of note with this example are:

(i) The sum of the costs allocated against each cost centre is equal to the aggregate figures presented in Figure 3.7. To illustrate this consider the example of the wages and salaries budget.

	Consolidated Format	Cost Centred Format
Swimming Pool	N/A	63 000
Sports Hall	N/A	35 000
Bar Catering	N/A	30 000
Total	128 000	128 000

The major implication of the essential need for figures to reconcile, is that the management and financial accounts must be drawn from the same system. Parallel finance systems are doomed to inevitable failure.

(ii) It is possible to identify the performance of each cost centre relative to its own budget and also relative to the other cost centres.

Using the imaginary figures from above, management are now in a position to consider each cost centre in turn – an opportunity which was not possible when all the figures are presented in summary form. Typical qualitative explanations for each cost centre are indicated below.

Swimming pool
The key reason for this cost centre not meeting its targets is a shortfall in income of £20,000. The manager has tried to rectify this by a package of cost savings on all budgets, but the net result has been to make a loss of £2,000 rather than the budgeted surplus of £2,800.

Sports hall
Despite a failure to meet the budgeted income target by £5,000, expenditure savings have enabled the sports hall to contribute a surplus of £1,500 rather than the planned deficit of £4,800.

Bar and catering
Even though sales have been more than anticipated, costs have increased proportionately more than income. This has resulted in a £1,500 reduction in the surplus that was budgeted for.

The overall position is that the centre has met its targets but two cost centres have failed to meet their budgets. Clearly, had the underperforming cost centres met their targets, then the actual surplus would have been greater than the £5,000 planned for. In the end, the surplus from the sports hall has been used to write off under performance in other areas.

Not only is it possible to quantify that there has been a series of variances, but it is also possible to identify where the variances have occurred. This enables managers to make more specific decisions about how to control their business as effectively as possible. This compares as infinitely more favourable to taking ill-informed general decisions.

(iii) It is possible to use information from cost centring to help managers set prices more rationally. Price setting should be based on three important factors: firstly, the cost of provision; secondly, the potential demand; and, thirdly, the objectives of the organisation. Taking this theory to its logical conclusion, it is impossible to set prices rationally without identifying the component costs of any product or service. Cost-based pricing, as one dimension to pricing decisions, is a far more logical approach than the highly popular method of "copy-cat" pricing which merely imitates what is being charged elsewhere.

Practical applications of cost centring

For any organisation which provides more than one kind of product or service, it is desirable to know the real performance of each one in isolation. The only practical way in which this can be achieved is by the use of cost centres. Leisure activities tend to demonstrate demand for different services as a part of the same experience. For example, a night at the theatre may entail some of the following expenses: parking fees, theatre tickets, pre-show drinks, a programme, ice creams or sweets, interval drinks and a post-show meal. Good managers will have financial expectations of each cost centre and will want to analyse the performance of each cost centre as well as the business overall.

The practical application of cost centring in leisure can be illustrated by looking at a range of different facilities and the types of cost centre which are often found in them, as illustrated in Table 3.1.

Sports Centre	Hotel	Theatre	Bowling Alley
"Wet" side	Accommodation	Box Office	Admission
"Dry" side	Restaurant	Programmes	Bowling charges
Health suite	Bars	Catering	Slot Machines
Vending	Room service	Bars	Catering
Other sales	Souvenirs	Confectionery	Merchandising

Table 3.1

Problems with cost centring

Unfortunately, cost centring often does not happen in leisure, despite its obvious advantages to management. The main reasons for this divergence between management theory and management practice can be explained by three major problems:

(i)   A finance system that cannot cope with cost centring;

(ii) An inability to allocate costs accurately;

(iii) An unwillingness by budget controllers to accept greater accountability.

Overcoming the problems with cost centring

In reality these three problems are to a certain extent dependent upon one another. However, in the interests of simplicity, it is possible to illustrate each problem area on its own.

(i) *Finance systems*

A finance system which permits cost centres to be identified as part of the overall accounting process requires proper planning. The first question managers need to ask themselves is "How would we like to see our financial information presented?" Once a clear model has been established, it is then possible to construct a reporting system that will achieve this. Too often the constraint is that managers are unable or unwilling to alter an existing system regardless of its obvious inadequacies.

The practical solution to inadequate finance systems is contained in the heart of the statutory financial system called the "nominal" or "general" ledger. In effect each income or expenditure type has its own name or account against which transactions are entered. Thus in a cost centre reporting system there will need to be more account headings than under traditional systems.

For internal purposes, this permits information to be presented in a way which is helpful to management. For external purposes, the same information can be consolidated to meet audit requirements.

Example

Consider the case of a sports centre which reports its performance in four cost centres and wishes to analyse, for example, electricity usage. The potential contrast in systems is shown below.

Budget Heading: Electricity	Traditional Format	Cost Centred Format
"Wet" side	Not possible	12 000
"Dry" side	Not possible	7 250
Trading	Not possible	2 500
Administration	Not Possible	1 250
Total	33 250	33 250

If the same coding format was applied to every account, then it can be seen that a cost-centred system would need (in the example above) four times as many budget codes as a traditional system. To cost centre reports efficiently for even a small to medium-sized organisation, normally requires the use of a computerised nominal ledger system.

This has three major benefits for the leisure manager: firstly, it is possible to have an almost infinite number of budget codes; secondly, errors can be minimised by being identified at the input stage (i.e. entries which do not balance cannot be entered); and, thirdly, the computer can be configured to produce the output in any way that managers require.

(ii) *Allocating costs accurately*

The allocation of costs against cost centres is often cited as a reason for not using them. There is a false perception that some costs cannot be allocated accurately. This is not the case in practice and merely requires a little application and experimentation to succeed.

Example 1: wages

Imagine the case of a part-time member of staff who works as a pool attendant, gymnasium coach and relief bar worker. It is appropriate that their gross wages be charged against the cost centre in which they have worked. This is easily solved by adapting a time sheet to provide all the information that is required, as illustrated in Figure 3.8.

Cost Centred Time Sheet

Staff Name:

Week Ending: Saturday 11th June 1994

Day	Wet	Dry	Bar	Other	Total
Sun					OFF
Mon	8-4 7hrs				7hrs
Tue		12-8 7hrs	8-11 3hrs		10hrs
Wed		12-6 5hrs	6-9 3hrs		8hrs
Thurs					OFF
Fri	7-12 5hrs	12-3 3hrs			8hrs
Sat		12-6 6hrs	6-9 3hrs		9hrs
Total	12hrs	21hrs	9hrs		42hrs
Rate	£4.00	£5.00	£3.50		
Pay	48.00	105.00	31.50		184.50

Approved.................... Position......................

Figure 3.8 Cost-centred time sheet

The wages are an essential item to cost centre since typically they account for the highest proportion of expenditure – in some cases as much as 80% of the overall total.

Example 2: fixed costs

A potentially more difficult case is allocating fixed costs, such as the uniform business rate, to cost centres. However, this and other fixed costs are relatively straightforward to allocate by using a floor space percentage model. Imagine the rates for a building are £15,000 and the four cost centres take up the following spaces:

	Area	Rates	Cost-Centred Rates
"Wet" side	35%	15 000	5 250
"Dry" side	25%	15 000	3 750
Trading	20%	15 000	3 000
Administration	20%	15 000	3 000
		Total	15 000

The amount of rates chargeable to a given cost centre can be allocated rationally using the floor space as the criterion.

Example 3: variable costs

Costs such as water, photocopying or telephone should be allocated on a direct usage basis. It is obvious that the "wet" side of a sports centre will use more water than the "dry" side and this imbalance should be reflected accordingly.

There are two ways that this can be done effectively. The first technique would be for the centre to install separate meters for each cost centre. This is the best idea in theory and is a technique that is used in rented accommodation or in leisure facilities where, for example, catering facilities are provided by an external contractor. Often cost-centred metering is not possible or cost-effective. This can be overcome by the second technique, which is to use rational experimentation to determine the amount of a bill to allocate to a cost centre. For allocating electricity costs from a single invoice, it would make sense to calculate the electrical rating of each cost centre as a method of cost allocation. The total bill could then be divided amongst the cost centres by the appropriate proportion. Refinement could take place by conducting a limited in-house survey to estimate the usage patterns by each department. The important point is that cost centring will not lead to an increase in absolute expenditure. Thus if the initial allocations are not quite accurate enough, then the budget can be modified to become more reflective of what is actually happening.

To prevent cost centre managers from introducing their own agendas to the experimental stage, a "no virements" rule can be introduced to all shared variable costs. This enables a given timespan's performance to be monitored clearly, so that in subsequent budgets the allocation of variable costs is as accurate as is reasonably possible.

Many items of common usage such as telephones or photocopiers can have their expenditure monitored by the use of simple cost-centring techniques. These include: itemised telephone bills for each extension and the use of a key counter to measure how many photocopies an individual cost centre has made. This enables greater clarity in the measuring of the actual costs attributable to a given cost centre.

(iii) *Management and staff resistance*

The greater accountability that cost centring brings can often be met by concern and even resistance by staff. Often the major reasons for this is that the introduction of change (in this case cost centring) is communicated badly to staff, or actual versus budget comparisons become a substitute for proper performance appraisal.

The primary solution to this is for the introduction of change and the justification for it, to be thought out and implemented in a participative manner. If people feel involved in change and can see precisely why it is being implemented, then they are far more likely to be positive towards it. On a secondary level, performance appraisal must focus on the individual and not the budget. Financial information does not tell us everything that we need to know.

Example

Who is doing the better job out of an imaginary pair of maintenance staff? Person A has £1000 underspent on their budget but the venue is covered in graffiti and has numerous light bulbs that are not working. Person B has £250 overspent on their budget and the venue is in pristine condition.

By seeing the wider angle of individual performance, it is possible to avoid making the mistake of judging people solely by the "bottom line".

Summary

The aim of this chapter has been to highlight some areas of good practice in the reporting of financial information. The major requirements for financial information are that it should be presented in a format that is clear, easily understood by the untrained eye and informative. There is no set way of presenting financial data. The onus is on management to present data in a manner which is appropriate to the needs of the organisation. This means being aware of the basic principles of financial reporting and applying them sensibly.

As figures do not reveal the full picture of financial performance, it is not good practice to rely on quantitative information alone. In reality, this means that managers have two major responsibilities when presenting financial data: firstly, to identify the magnitude of budgetary variances; and, secondly, to explain clearly the significance (if any) of these variances. Often it is the latter of these tasks which is more difficult. However, by being in control of your business, i.e. making sensible decisions on the basis of financial information, these difficulties can be overcome relatively easily.

Review and management applications

Having grasped the basic points from this chapter you should now consider the following questions in the context of your own working environment.

(1) Is the financial information that you require presented in a way which can be easily understood even by the non-financial manager?

(2) What constraints do you encounter which prevent information from being accurate and timely?

(3) How, in practice, do you analyse financial statements and, in particular, variances? Can you distinguish between actual and timing variances?

(4) What would be the likely consequences of you trying to introduce expenditure control sheets and cost centring as a way of allocating increased responsibility to staff?

(5) Are the merits of cost centring worth the additional costs that might be incurred by presenting your financial information in such a way?

Further reading

Riddle, G. (1983) *Stage One Cost Accounting*, Northwick Publishers, Worcester.

Tilley, C. and Whitehouse, J. (1992) *Finance and Leisure*, Longman/ILAM, Harlow.

Cook, P. (1993) *Local Authority Financial Management and Accounting*, Longman, Harlow.

Chapter 4
Cost behaviour and management implications

Objectives

The objective of this chapter is to illustrate the practical applications of cost behaviour in leisure management. Understanding how costs behave will enable managers to make rational decisions in the following management situations:

(i) The effects of differing marketing policies;

(ii) Special offers and group discounts;

(iii) Break-even calculations;

(iv) Cost-based pricing decisions;

(v) Cost structures.

These all seem like obvious items of everyday management that can be taken care of by using common sense. To a limited extent this is true, but common sense and experience should be underpinned by some basic principles. Unfortunately, these are often clouded by jargon that deters even the most conscientious manager from coming to grips with them. The aim of this chapter is to demonstrate the principles with some typical leisure examples, and to demystify the jargon.

Having understood the basics of costing, it then becomes possible to begin examining the effects of budgeting for differing levels of service or output. A further management application of costing is to model the budgetary consequences of changes to some of the key variables, i.e. what would the effect on the bottom line be of a 10% increase in salaries? This is known in management accounting terms as "sensitivity analysis" and is discussed at the end of the chapter.

1 Types of cost and their behaviour

Leisure is predominantly a service industry and thus many management text books written about production management do not contain directly transferable principles. However, in all costing exercises, the important distinction to make in terms of costs are between those which are fixed and those which are variable. A third category of cost exists called semi-variable, semi-fixed or step costs which contain an element of both fixed and variable costs.

Fixed costs
A fixed cost is a type of expenditure which does not vary in the short term in proportion to the level of output. For example, if the insurance for a cinema is £2,000

---

per year, then it will remain at this level whether there are 100 or 100,000 admissions per year. This can be shown graphically as shown in Graph 1. Fixed costs remain stable in the short-term but do fluctuate in the longer term, e.g. insurance premiums normally increase annually.

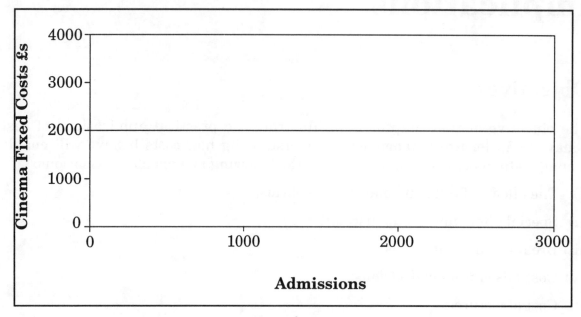

Graph 1: Fixed costs

Other examples of fixed costs include: salaries, uniform business rates, rent charges, water rates and professional fees.

Variable costs

A variable cost is an expense which varies in direct proportion to the level of output. In cinemas it is normal to pay a percentage of box office receipts to the film distributor as a charge for film hire. The more admissions a venue makes, the more money it takes and the more it pays in film hire. This can be represented by both a table and a graph. Assume that the average price of a cinema ticket is £4.00 and the film hire percentage is 30%. Table 4.1 below represent the weekly admissions of a typical cinema. See also Graph 2.

Admissions	Price	Revenue	Film Hire (30%)	Gross Profit (70%)
1,000	£4.00	4,000	1,200	2,800
1,600	£4.00	6,400	1,920	4,480
1,800	£4.00	7,200	2,160	5,040
2,400	£4.00	9,600	2,880	6,720
3,000	£4.00	12,000	3,600	5,280

Table 4.1

Another expression for a variable cost is a marginal cost, i.e. the cost of making one more admission or how much would be saved by making one less admission.

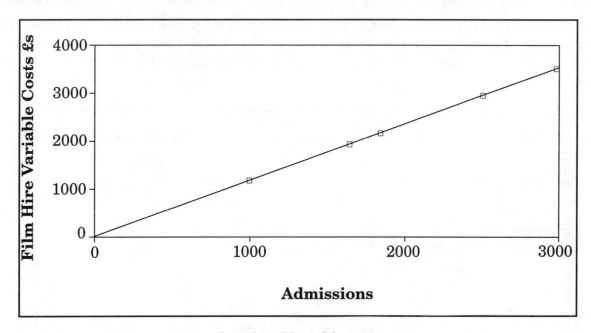

Graph 2: Variable costs

Semi-variable costs

A semi-variable or semi-fixed cost is a type of expense which contains elements of both fixed and variable cost types. As an example, the licensing conditions of a cinema may stipulate that there must be a minimum of four ushers on duty at all times up to 1,000 admissions and then one further usher per additional 600 customers thereafter. Using the admissions data above and assuming that each usher costs £30 per day, the semi-variable nature of this cost can be demonstrated. It is also assumed that the cinema is open 7 days per week to compute the weekly cost. See Table 4.2 and Graph 3.

Admissions	Ushers	Rate/Day	Cost/Day	Cost/Week
1,000	4	£30	120	840
1,600	5	£30	150	1050
1,800	5	£30	150	1050
2,400	6	£30	180	1260
3,000	7	£30	210	1470

Table 4.2

Managers need to exercise discretion when deciding what categories to place costs in. For example, many textbooks cite the telephone as an example of a semi-variable cost, i.e. there is the quarterly line rental (fixed) plus the additional charge of call units (variable). Using cost behaviour sensibly requires managers to identify the important variables and what actually affects them.

This may vary from one context to another. For example, if managers were seeking to reduce telephone costs, then clearly the telephone is a semi-variable cost. However, in the context of looking at admissions, telephone charges will not vary in accordance with the number of people using a facility. The pragmatic solution is to say that the telephone has a fixed budget of, say, £200 per quarter. In the context of total admissions, telephone charges would be included with the other fixed costs.

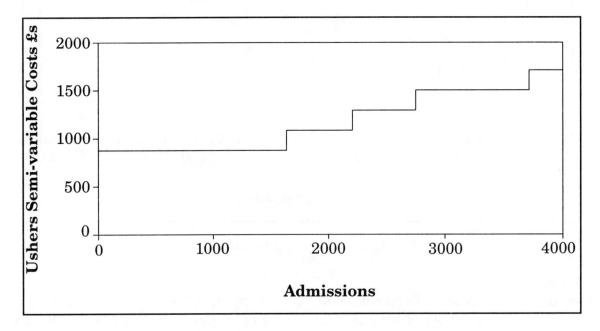

Graph 3: Semi-variable costs

Total costs
The three types of cost can be combined to show (in Table 4.3) how costs vary in accordance with variables such as sales or admissions. Assume that fixed costs are £2,000 per week.

Admissions	0	1 000	1 600	1 800	2 400	3 000
Revenue	0	4 000	6 400	7 200	9 600	12 000
Fixed Costs	–2 000	–2 000	–2 000	–2 000	–2 000	–2 000
Variable Costs						
Film Hire	0	–1 200	-1 920	-2 160	-2 880	–3 600
Semi Variable						
Ushers	0	–840	–1 050	–1 050	–1 260	–1 470
Total Costs	–2 000	–4 040	–4 970	–5 210	–6 140	–7 070
Profit/Loss	–2 000	-40	1 430	1 990	3 460	4 930

Table 4.3

All three types of costs and the total cost can be combined on the same graph (see Graph 4) to give an indication of overall or total cost behaviour.

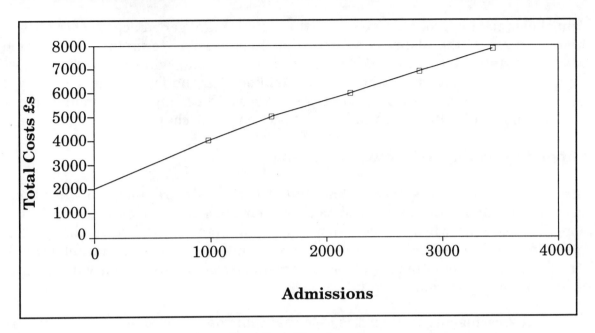

Graph 4: Total costs

Unit costs

Note how so far all of the cost relationships have resulted in straight lines. However, if we were to look at the unit cost of each admission at the various admission levels, the picture would be entirely different. The resulting graph would be curved and indicate that the average unit cost decreases as admissions increase but NOT in direct proportion. (See Graph 5.)

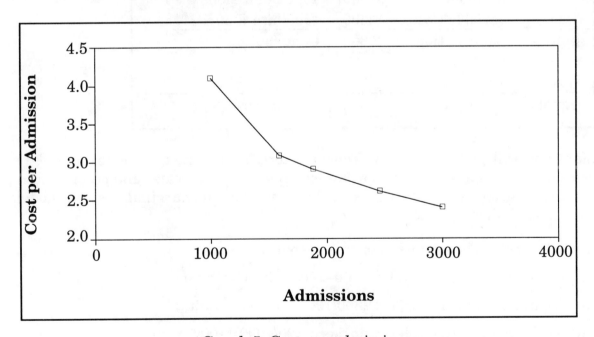

Graph 5: Cost per admission

Admissions	0	1 000	1 600	1 800	2 400	3 000
Total Costs	−2 000	−4 040	−4 970	−5 210	−6 140	−7 070
Cost/Admission	N/A	£4.04	£3.11	£2.89	£2.56	£2.36

Using basic costing procedures such as these gives managers a degree of control of their business at the planning stage. It becomes possible to predict for example how many staff are required on duty and how much they will cost. Perhaps most importantly, if management know what the likely demand for a given service will be, then they can use cost data to help set prices. These and other management applications will be illustrated in the next section of the chapter.

2 Applying costing to leisure management

Businesses in all sectors need to know what their costs are and also what their costs will be under different conditions. Often marketing strategies are based along a continuum which ranges from "pile them high and sell them cheap", e.g. Amstrad satellite dishes, to a policy of premium pricing, e.g. upmarket private health clubs. All too often, vital management decisions are taken without due regard to the implications of cost.

Before progressing any further it is essential that the expression "contribution" is understood. When referring to marginal costing examples, contribution is defined as the selling price minus the variable (marginal) cost. Whatever is left over is said be a contribution to the fixed costs of the business. Using data from the cinema example we can illustrate this numerically.

At 1000 admissions:

	Revenue	4,000	1000 admissions @ £4
less	Variable Costs	1,200	Film hire @ 30%
equals	Contribution	2,800	Contribution
less	Fixed Costs	2,840	Fixed Costs
equals	Profit/(Loss)	(40)	Profit/(Loss)

Managers will probably already know the term contribution as "gross profit", i.e. sales minus cost of sales. The obvious examples are bars, cafes and other vending activities in leisure venues. The basic layout for all marginal costing models should be as shown in the box above.

Contribution can be expressed in any one of three ways:

(i)   As an absolute amount, i.e. 4000–1200 = 2800 in total;

(ii) As an amount per unit, i.e. 2800/1000 = 2.80 per unit;

(iii) As the contribution/sales ratio, i.e. (2800/4000)*100% = 70%.

A further relationship to understand is that between contribution and net profit. Assuming that fixed costs remain the same, then it follows logically that the higher the contribution, the higher the profit (or the lower the loss). This too can be demonstrated using the cinema data.

		Admissions		Difference
		1600	1800	200
	Revenue	6400	7200	800
less	Variable Costs	1920	2160	240
equals	Contribution	4480	5040	560
less	Fixed Costs	3050	3050	0
equals	Profit/(Loss)	1430	1990	560

When fixed costs remain the same, then extra contribution equals extra profit. Understanding the relationship between these variables is essential to applying marginal costing.

How can marginal costing be used to help the leisure manager?

Example 1: marketing or pricing strategies
An introductory use of marginal costing can be seen by comparing different types of marketing strategies. A rock music promoter is seeking to maximise profit on an outdoor event and wishes to find out the best marketing strategy to adopt. Three options are available and the promoter is interested in the one which is the most profitable. Assume that fixed costs are the same for the three levels of service.

Option 1
An economy show with limited special effects, no support band and an inferior quality sound system. The variable cost would be £7 per person, sales are estimated at 6,000 with ticket prices of £13.

Option 2
A value for money show with a support band and a good quality sound system. The variable cost would be £8 per person, sales are estimated at 5,500 with ticket prices of £16.

Option 3
A premium show with little or no expense spared. The variable cost would be £10 per person, sales are estimated at 4,900 with ticket prices of £20.

Solution

		Low	Mid	High
	Admissions	6 000	5 500	4 900
	Price	£13	£16	£20
	Variable cost	£7	£8	£12
	Revenue	78 000	88 000	98 000
less	Variable costs	42 000	44 000	58 800
equals	Contribution	36 000	44 000	39 200

As the fixed costs are the same, then highest contribution equals highest profit and thus the promoter would be advised to pursue the "value for money" mid-price option.

The importance of contribution can be seen from a more mainstream leisure example – the local authority swimming pool. It is difficult to think of costs which vary in proportion to the number of swimmers so let us assume that variable costs are zero, fixed costs are £2,500 per week and that opening hours remain the same. The possible pricing strategies are 2,000 admissions per week at £2, or 1,800 admissions per week at £2.25.

		Option 1	Option 2
	Admissions	2000	1800
	Price	£2.00	£2.25
	Variable cost	nil	nil
	Revenue	4000	4050
less	Variable Costs	0	0
equals	Contribution	4000	4050
less	Fixed Costs	2500	2500
equals	Profit	1500	1550

Zero or very low variable costs are very common in the leisure industry, e.g. theme parks, hotel rooms, health clubs and so on. This means that leisure managers need to be particularly aware of contribution and the role it plays in meeting financial objectives. In the swimming pool example above, if the objectives are to maximise participation, then Option 1 is preferable. If the objective is to maximise profit, then Option 2 is preferable.

Whatever pricing or marketing strategies are selected, they should be internally consistent with the objectives of the organisation. Any decision which is made rationally and can be justified shows good budgetary control. When decisions are made without regard to the underlying logic, then managers leave themselves open to criticism. The rational way to control is to perform the necessary calculations and then select the outcome which is most consistent with what you wish to achieve.

Example 2: group discounts and special offers
One of the distinctive features of service industries is that the product cannot be stored. If a charter flight aeroplane takes off with 20 empty seats, then those seats are lost for ever. Equally if a theatre is half full for a performance, the unsold seats cannot be sold at some time in the future. An understanding of how the concept of contribution works can give an insight into special offers such as cheap holidays and the common practice of negotiating discounts in hotels.

Consider the case of a charter flight to a holiday destination. The plane has a capacity of 300 seats at a standard price of £150 per seat. The variable costs of fuel, in-flight meals and landing taxes are £45 per passenger. There is an additional fixed cost or overhead charge of £11,500 per flight. Why do seats on this aeroplane sometimes appear in advertisements for £100?

The answer lies in the relationship between contribution and unfilled capacity. If all of the seats have not been sold, then the management have two options: either do nothing and lose any potential revenue, or try to obtain at least some form of contribution from the unsold seats. Imagine that 25 seats remain unsold.

Scenario 1: do nothing

		Full Price
	Seats Sold	275
	Price	150
	Variable Cost	45
	Revenue	41 250
less	Variable Costs	12 375
equals	Contribution	28 875
less	Fixed Costs	11 500
equals	Profit	17 375

Scenario 2: discount unsold seats

		Full Price	Discount	Totals
	Seats Sold	275	25	
	Price	150	100	
	Variable cost	45	45	
	Revenue	41250	2500	43750
less	Variable Costs	12375	1125	13500
equals	Contribution	28875	1375	30250
less	Fixed Costs	11500	0	11500
equals	Profit	17375	1365	18750

Again, there is further proof that when fixed costs remain the same, then extra contribution equals extra profit. This can now help to explain why it is possible to negotiate discounts with hotels, for example. If a hotelier does not sell a room, then the potential revenue from that room is lost for ever. Thus, if a customer offers a sum of money which more than covers the variable cost of the room, then the hotelier will get at least some contribution towards the hotel's fixed costs.

As an extreme example, the concept of contribution and unfilled capacity can explain why theatres often "paper" performances with low attendance. ("Paper" means to give away free tickets in order to create the illusion of a respectable number of people in the audience.) If the performance is on a fee basis, then there are no variable costs. Thus giving tickets away is not illogical. Those who have been given tickets may buy programmes, ice creams or drinks, all of which will make some additional contribution to other cost centres. However, caution must be exercised when discounting. It is vital that discounting is used selectively and on target markets, otherwise the risk of devaluing the product is a real threat.

If managers are aware of their fixed and variable costs, then they are in a position to cost accurately the effects of discounting and special offers. All too often, these decisions are based on intuition rather than a process of pro-active budgetary control. Using basic costing theory can help to overcome this.

Example 3: break-even calculations

All businesses, regardless of the sector in which they operate, have one common requirement, i.e. they must work within the financial resources which have been allocated to them. In the private sector, although the overall aim is to make a profit, it is unlikely that the business will fail if profits are less than anticipated. Where businesses are likely to fail is when they start to make losses. The same concept can be modified for the non-profit sector. In most publicly provided leisure organisations, the selling price is lower than the cost. This is fine in principle if there is sufficient agreed subsidy to cover these losses. What jeopardises public leisure organisations is the scenario in which managers spend more than their allocated subsidy. Businesses which operate outside of their financial resources also tend to make extreme decisions which in turn contributes to an unpleasant working environment. Thus a vital piece of information that managers require is to know the point at which making losses will be avoided. This is known as the break-even point, which can be defined as "the minimum level of business required to avoid making a loss".

This can be illustrated by the use of a simple example.

Consider the case of a cinema which has the following weekly targets:

Number of admissions	1,200
Average ticket price	£4 per seat
Film hire (variable cost)	25% of revenue
Fixed costs	£1,500

Using this data it becomes possible to identify the break-even point, i.e. the point below which it is costing the manager money to open the front doors!

	Budget	Break-even	Loss-making
Admissions	1200	500	475
Revenue (£4 head)	4800	2000	1900
Variable Costs (Film Hire)	1200	500	475
Contribution	3600	1500	1425
Fixed Costs	1500	1500	1500
Profit/(Loss)	2100	0	(75)

The points to extract from this example are as follows:

(i) The fixed costs have not altered in response to the changes in the level of admissions.

(ii) The change in profits or losses equals the change in the amount of contribution. Examine the case of the break-even and loss-making columns to prove this, i.e. the £75 reduction in contribution results in the break even position changing to a loss of £75.

(iii) We can refine the definition of the break-even point and place it in a numerical context. The break-even point is defined as the point at which the contribution equals the fixed costs. This can be seen clearly by looking at the break-even column above.

The break-even point and information deficiencies.
The example above is perfectly simple but relies on one major assumption, i.e. managers have all of the necessary information at their disposal. Often this is not the case.

Example (a): sales required to break-even
A small holiday operator has 20 apartments which are hired out at £240 per week and which have a marginal cost of £90 per week each. The fixed costs are calculated as being £2,100 per week. What is the break-even point?

Revenue per apartment	240
Marginal cost per apartment	90
Contribution per apartment	150 (or unit contribution)
Fixed costs	2100

The answer to this problem lies in the relationship between the unit contribution and the fixed costs. The number of unit contributions required to break even is the same as the number of sales required to break-even. Thus the number of apartments which need to be rented out each week simplifies down to:

$$\frac{\text{Fixed Costs}}{\text{Unit Contribution}} = \frac{2100}{150} = 14 \text{ apartments per week}$$

Example (b): breaking-even when unit data is not available

Often in leisure management, venues have bars or other trading outlets to take advantage of secondary spending. Using a bar as an example, it would be impractical to use a basic marginal costing matrix for every different product which was sold. It would be impossible to calculate the precise range of drinks that need to be sold to break-even. This is where the importance of the contribution to sales ratio (C/S ratio) discussed at the start of the chapter can be used.

A bar has an average turnover of £5,000 per week and an average gross profit of 45%. The fixed costs allocated against the bar as a cost centre are £1,760 per week. What level of business is required to break-even? In this case it is not appropriate to look for a permutation of products to be sold but rather an absolute amount of money.

Sales	5,000	100%
less		
Cost of sales (marginal cost)	2,250	45%
equals		
Contribution	2,750	55% (C/S ratio)
less		
Fixed costs	1,760	
equals		
Profit	990	

The solution to this example hinges on the relationship between the contribution to sales ratio and fixed costs. For every £1 taken over the bar, £0.55 is available as contribution to the fixed costs. The number of contributions per pound of revenue needed to pay the fixed costs is also the number of pounds revenue needed. This simplifies down to:

$$\frac{\text{Fixed Costs}}{\text{C/S Ratio}} = \frac{1760}{0.55} = 3,200 \text{ worth of bar sales per week}$$

Typically, real life will not necessarily go to plan and thus it is always important to be prepared for different scenarios than were originally anticipated. In the bar example above, the level of profitability appears to be acceptable at £5,000 per week. But at what point do managers need to exercise considerable control to prevent the business from making losses? By performing the break-even calculation and deriving a minimal level of business required, managers can use this vital threshold to control the business. Thus if business were slack, managers could try to reduce other costs to try and bring what is happening more in line with what was planned. Put simply, if you are unable to make any money, then you should at least try to save some. In this case, maybe use less staff hours.

Example 4: cost-based pricing decisions

Why is it more expensive to watch Manchester United play a Premier League football match than it is to watch Rotherham United play a Second Division match? There are a number of different but related answers to this question. One, however, is obvious. Manchester United have higher costs and therefore need to charge higher prices to cover these costs. This is the basic logic behind cost-based pricing decisions and is far more scientific than simply copying what others are charging.

There are two basic questions that all managers need to ask themselves when considering financial management: firstly, is the selling price higher than the cost?; and, secondly, is the business well set to continue trading? These questions are applicable across all sectors by interpreting the first question as "is the organisation working within the resources allocated to it?" In basic terms this recognises that in the public sector the selling price may be lower than the economic cost but there is an agreed subsidy to cover the shortfall.

To illustrate the point, consider the case of a private sector leisure pool and a local authority "traditional" pool. A breakdown of their costs is shown below. The private sector pool is committed to a minimum profit of £70,000, the public sector pool enjoys a subsidy of £50,000. If prices were based on cost, what would they be?

	Private Pool	Public Pool
Annual admissions	65,000	52,000
Total costs	125,000	128,000
Financial objective	30,000	–50,000
Cost per Swim	125,000/65,000	128,000/52,000
	= £1.92	= £2.46

The price can be easily worked for both cases using simple equations.

Private pool price = 65,000(X) – 125,000 = 70,000
where (X) is the price required to give a profit of £70,000.

Solving for (X) gives the following answer:

	65,000(X)	- 125,000	=	70,000
Step 1 add 125,000		+ 125,000	=	+125,000
	65,000(X)		=	195,000
Step 2 divide by 65,000	(X)		=	195,000/65,000
	(X)		=	£3.00

Public pool price = 52,000(X) – 128,000 = -50,000

	52,000(X)	- 128,000	=	-50,000
Step 1 add 128,000		+ 128,000	=	+128,000
	52,000(X)		=	78,000
Step 2 divide by 52,000	(X)		=	78,000/52,000
	(X)		=	£1.50

For both examples, the common denominator for setting the price has been to relate the price to cost. Price, in the first instance, has been set on the basis of internal factors, i.e. costs and attendances rather than external factors which are largely irrelevant, e.g. competitors. Because the public sector pool has a subsidy, the selling price has resulted in being less than the cost. This is totally justifiable as long as it meets the objectives of the provider and the organisation operates within the allocated subsidy.

Only when a base level of price has been established on the basis of cost does it make sense to consider other variables such as demand. No sensible manager will sell a service at less price than they can afford to, so clearly a detailed knowledge of costs is a vital starting point in the pricing process.

Rational pricing decisions should be based on three sets of considerations: firstly, the actual cost of providing a given service; secondly, the anticipated demand for a given service; and, thirdly, the objectives of the organisation providing the service. All three factors are linked and should be used whenever pricing decisions are made rather than the disturbingly common practice of "copy-cat" pricing. The technique of leisure managers going out to rival venues and noting down their prices with a view to basing their own on these is totally illogical. Pricing should be well thought out rather than "we should be 50p cheaper than whatever the Odeon are charging".

If you base your prices on those of your competitors, then you are making the tacit assumption that your costs, level of demand and objectives are the same or similar. The likelihood of this being the case will only ever be the result of a coincidence. It is not within the scope of this book to discuss demand theory nor objectives but the starting points in any pricing decision must be:

(i)   How much does this service cost to provide?

(ii) How many people are likely to want to buy it?

(iii) What do we wish to achieve by providing it?

This three-stage model is applicable to all sectors as it is equally appropriate to non-profit as well as profit-making leisure organisations.

As a way of illustrating the three determinants of price, consider the case of a touring theatre performance which has been booked into two different types of venue for one performance only. One is a private sector theatre with a brief to maximise profits. The other is local authority theatre which is subsidised on account of its wider social brief. The likely costs and demand patterns are presented below. The objective is to try and arrive at a cost based price for each venue on the basis of the data provided. Assume that the cost of booking the performance is 35% of total receipts or £3,500, whichever is the greater.

	Private Theatre	Public Theatre
Capacity	2000	2000
Demand	1200	2000
Price per seat	unknown	unknown
Marginal cost per seat	35%	35%
Fixed costs	2800	6450
Financial objective	+6000	Break-even

Possible outcomes are illustrated below indicating pricing levels for both organisations which would also enable them to meet their stated objectives.

Private Theatre			
Quantity	Unit ↓		Total ↓
Sales	Price		Revenue
1200	×	11.50	= 13,800
	Unit Variable Cost		Total Variable Cost
1200	×	4.03	4,830
	Unit Contribution		Total Contribution
1200	×	7.47	8,970
	Fixed Costs		(2,800)
	Profit		6,170

The important factors to note here are that the bottom line minimum profit of £6,000 has been met and also the total variable costs are more than the minimum guarantee figure of £3,500.

```
Public Theatre

Quantity                        Unit                    Total
                                 ↓                        ↓
Sales                          Price                   Revenue
2000            ×               5.00      =            10,000
                                Unit                    Total
                            Variable Cost          Variable Cost
2000            ×               1.75                    3,500

                            Contribution           Contribution
2000            ×               3.25                    6,500

                            Fixed Costs               (6,450)
                               Profit                      50
```

Note how in addition to meeting the minimum guarantee figure and the minimum bottom line of breaking-even, the theatre has also met the social objective of encouraging participation, i.e. 800 more admissions than the private sector.

How are the suggested prices arrived at?
In practice there are two ways that managers can use the variables at their disposal to deduce a logical price. Firstly, using the relationship between variable cost, contribution and fixed costs, it is possible to model the matrix above using trial and error. A second and more useful technique is by customising a computer spreadsheet to create your own model. If you look at the calculations which are required, there is nothing more complicated than multiplication and subtraction. This sort of simple model lends itself to being produced on a spreadsheet. An advantage of using spreadsheets is that when one variable is altered, those which are dependent upon it will change automatically. The use of spreadsheets in solving real world problems is shown in Chapter five.

Example 5: cost structures in leisure
The answer to the second basic financial management question, i.e. "is the business well set to continue trading?", can be understood in part by looking at cost structures. An alternative way of asking this question is to evaluate the extent to which an organisation is capable of surviving a downturn in the level of business. From most of the costing examples it can be seen that generally there is a combination of both fixed and variable costs. Cost structure is the term given to the proportion of each type of cost as a function of total costs. For planning purposes, this is an essential piece of information to be aware of.

To illustrate this point, imagine the case of an investor who has to choose between buying a hotel or a restaurant. Prior to making any decision, the investor analyses the cost structures of each option and these are shown below.

Base Case	Hotel	Restaurant
Revenue	405,000	405,000
less		
Variable costs	101,250 (25%)	283,500 (70%)
equals		
Contribution	303,750	121,500
less		
Fixed costs	263,250	81,000
equals		
Profit	40,500	40,500

Both options appear to be offering the same profit, but they are not equally placed to withstand a down turn in the level of expected business. This can be proved by simulating the effects of a 10% fall in the level of budgeted business.

−10% Scenario	Hotel	Restaurant
Revenue	364,500	364,500
less		
Variable costs	91,125 (25%)	255,150 (70%)
equals		
Contribution	273,375	109,350
less		
Fixed costs	263,250	81,000
equals		
Profit	10,125	28,350

Clearly the effects are not identical. The budgeted profits for the hotel option have fallen from £40,500 to £10,125, i.e. 75%, whilst the restaurant's profits have fallen from £40,500 to £28,350, i.e. 30%. The reason for this is that the cost structures for each investment option are different. If an organisation fails to meet its targets, then the only costs which are saved are the variable or marginal costs. The fixed element of the costs (by definition) remains the same. Thus leisure organisations with high proportions of fixed costs are more vulnerable to downturns in trade than those in which variable costs are dominant.

This can be demonstrated by examining the proportion of fixed costs for each of the two options under the base case and −10% conditions.

	Hotel Base	%	Hotel −10%	%
Fixed	263,250	72%	263,500	74%
Variable	101,250	28%	91,125	26%
Total	364,500	100%	354,625	100%
Revenue	405,000		364,500	
Profit	40,500		10,125	

	Restaurant Base	%	Restaurant −10%	%
Fixed	81,000	22%	81,000	24%
Variable	283,500	78%	255,150	76%
Total	364,500	100%	336,150	100%
Revenue	405,000		364,500	
Profit	40,500		28,350	

At the base level, the total amount of costs are exactly the same but the proportion of fixed to variable costs is significantly different. The more sales reduce, the more fixed costs become an increasingly higher proportion of the total costs. However, there is a positive side to this relationship which is to consider the effects of an increase in the level of business for each option – for the sake of consistency assume 10%.

+10% Scenario	Hotel	Restaurant
Revenue less	445,500	445,500
Variable costs equals	111,375 (25%)	311,850 (70%)
Contribution less	334,125	133,650
Fixed costs equals	263,250	81,000
Profit	70,875	52,650

Under increasing levels of business conditions, the hotel shows a 43% increase in profits compared to the restaurant's 23%. Thus one of the major considerations for the investor is their own attitude towards future levels of business.

The practical application of cost structures
It is common practice in many leisure organisations to engage performers, celebrities or sports stars for contracts of work. Examples include theatre companies, pop groups, boxing matches and athletics events. The application of costing principles can help managers to share the risk of a promotion. There are normally two types of payment, either a flat fee or a share of the receipts generated by the event.

Example
A show targeted at families and children has been booked at a theatre for one performance. The performers require either a fee of £400 or 60% of the box office receipts. The theatre seats 400 and all tickets are sold at £3. Assume that fixed

costs of £250 are allocated against the performance. How could costing principles help to inform the management in their negotiations with the performers?

The first point to realise is that by agreeing to pay a flat fee of £400, management are committing themselves to a fixed cost and assuming all of the risk. By agreeing to a box office split arrangement, risk is shared but so is success. This can be modelled using a marginal costing matrix. The missing variable is the amount of revenue likely to be generated. Thus it is advisable to model various levels of business.

Flat Fee:

Audience	100	200	300	400
Price	£3	£3	£3	£3
Revenue	300	600	900	1200
less				
Variable cost	0	0	0	0
equals				
Contribution	300	600	900	1200
less				
Fixed Cost 1 (Fee)	400	400	400	400
Fixed Cost 2	250	250	250	250
equals				
Profit	−350	−50	250	550

Box Office Split:

Audience	100	200	300	400
Price	£3	£3	£3	£3
Revenue	300	600	900	1200
less				
Variable cost (60%)	180	360	540	720
equals				
Contribution	120	240	360	480
less				
Fixed Cost	250	250	250	250
equals				
Profit	−130	−10	110	230

The piece of information that the manager needs most is the point at which both options break-even. The break-even figure is calculated by using the contribution per unit and fixed costs relationship.

Fixed costs/contribution per unit = break-even units

For the fee option: 650/3.00 = 217 seats sold
For the box office split option: 250/1.20 = 209 seats sold

(Rounding is done to whole numbers as it is not possible to sell fractions of a seat!)

The monetary effect of various levels of business can be summarised as follows: extra contribution equals extra profit. For the flat fee option, every ticket sold above or below the break-even point will change the bottom line by £3. For the box office split option, every ticket sold above or below the break-even point will change the bottom line by £1.20.

Thus the final recommendation would be that up to 209 seats it is more cost-effective to select the box office split; beyond 217 seats the flat fee is preferable.

Further application of cost structures – the margin of safety
There is a recognised method to differentiate between, either, different businesses or different business proposals known as the "margin of safety". The margin of safety is simply a measure of the difference between the number of sales required to break-even and the number of sales which have been budgeted for. The principle behind this concept is that the greater the margin of safety, the more a business is likely to be able to survive adverse trading conditions.

This can be illustrated using the hotel and restaurant examples used at the start of this section.

Base Case	Hotel	Restaurant
Revenue	405,000	405,000
Variable costs	101,250 (25%)	283,500 (70%)
Contribution	303,750 (75%)	121,500 (30%)
Fixed costs	263,250	81,000
Break even sales	263,250/.75	81,000/.30
=	351,000	270,000
Budgeted sales =	405,000	405,000
Margin of safety	54,000	135,000
Profit	40,500	40,500

Naturally, for businesses which sell units, e.g. admissions, the margin of safety can be converted into the number of sales required rather than an absolute number.

The relationship between costs, sales, break-even and margin of safety can all be represented graphically using the data from the hotel and restaurant options, as in Graphs 6 and 7.

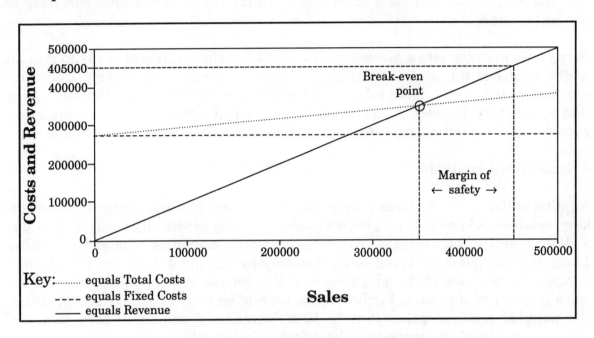

Graph 6   Hotel break-even chart

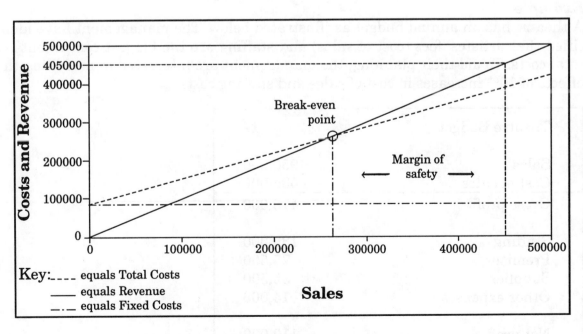

Graph 7   Restaurant break-even chart

3 Budgeting for differing levels of service

It is common practice to produce a budget for a given level of service, i.e. budgets are fixed. This does not mean that budgets do not or cannot change. Inevitably they will do if monitoring, review and virements are used. For managers who wish to control their businesses, it is important to realise how the financial components of a business relate to one another. This knowledge provides a valuable insight into the effects that increases or decreases in the levels of business will have on the bottom line.

Being able to anticipate a given scenario and have the strategies ready to react to it distinguishes the proactive manager from the glorified key holder. Control of business situations requires information and this is a further area for the application of costing principles. A fully worked example of a flexible budget plus a suggested computer spreadsheet template is illustrated in Chapter 5, Section 3.

4 Sensitivity analysis

An alternative method of examining how the bottom line adjusts to variations to key variables is known as sensitivity analysis. Using sensitivity analysis it is possible to identify the business essentials on which managers should be focusing. There is little point in trying to save money by clamping down on private telephone calls and use of the photocopier if the dominant components of costs are spiralling out of control. A further application of sensitivity analysis is to correct the popular misconception that "a 10% decrease in sales will lead to a 10% decrease in profit". By modelling the effects of what will happen if there is say a 10% increase in the cost of sales, managers will know where to concentrate their efforts.

Example
A theatre has an annual budget as illustrated below. The management have identified that artistes' fees (cost of sales) and staffing are the biggest components of total costs. To aid their planning, the management are interested in modelling the effects of 10% increases in cost of sales and staffing costs.

Theatre Budget	£s
Sales	950,000
Cost of sales	535,000
Gross profit	415,000
Staffing	180,000
Premises	75,500
Supplies	35,500
Other expenses	14,000
Net profit	110,000

Solution 1: 10% increase in artistes' fees

	Base Case	+10% Cost of Sales	Variance	Percentage Change
Sales	950,000	950,000	0	
Cost of sales	535,000	588,500	+53,500	+10%
Gross profit	415,000	361,500	−53,500	−13%
Staffing	180,000	180,000	0	
Premises	75,500	75,500	0	
Supplies	35,500	35,500	0	
Other expenses	14,000	14,000	0	
Net profit	110,000	56,500	−53,500	−49%

The effects of this scenario would be quite sobering to the venue management as they would realise how sensitive their bottom line is to increases in the cost of sales. With a 10% increase in cost of sales resulting in a 49% reduction in profits, management would be well advised to ensure that artistes' fees are kept within the allocated budget.

Solution 2: 10% increase in staffing costs

	Base Case	+10% Staffing	Variance	Percentage Change
Sales	950,000	950,000	0	
Cost of sales	535,000	535,000	0	
Gross profit	415,000	415,000	0	
Staffing	180,000	198,000	+18,000	+10%
Premises	75,500	75,500	0	
Supplies	35,500	35,500	0	
Other expenses	14,000	14,000	0	
Net profit	110,000	92,000	−18,000	−16%

Again, a 10% increase in staffing costs as a key variable has caused a disproportionate effect (−16%) to the bottom line. The use of a simple exercise such as this, provides conclusive evidence that cost of sales and staffing costs are the areas on which management should be concentrating the majority of their financial control. The sensitivity analyses shown above are no more than a practical application of cost structures outlined above in section 1 of this chapter. The only change is that the data has been presented in a format that managers may be more familiar with.

Summary

The focus of this chapter has been to apply basic costing theory and the issues arising from it in a manner that managers can relate to and will understand. Often the difficulty that managers have in applying costing theory is making the distinction between fixed and variable costs. This will vary in any given context. The question to ask yourself is: "Does this cost vary in direct proportion to the level of output?" If the answer is "yes", then the cost is variable and if "no" then it is fixed. In a service industry, such as leisure, it is quite typical for the proportion of fixed costs to be very high and in some cases 100%. Having the confidence to realise this should enable managers to use some of the principles arising from costing theory with confidence.

Review and management applications

This chapter has provided an overview of cost behaviour and its applications in practice. Having read the chapter you may wish to consider some of the following questions:

(1) Does your current management information system distinguish between fixed and variable costs?

(2) How are pricing decisions in your organisation made?

(3) How does this relate to logical pricing decisions based on cost, demand and organisational objectives?

(4) What are the implications of leisure venues typically having high fixed costs and low variable costs?

(5) How could a working knowledge of cost behaviour help you to do your job more rationally?

Further reading

Wilkinson-Riddle, G.J. and Patel, A. (1992) *Management Accounting Series Marginal Costing Software Manual*, Educational Software Products, Leicester.

Gratton, C. and Taylor, P. (1992) *Economics of Leisure Services Management*, Longman/ILAM, London.

Naylor, D. (1993) *Financial Control and Performance Measurement in Leisure and Recreation Management*, Ravenswood Publications Ltd, London.

Chapter 5
Spreadsheets, the manager's best friend?

Objectives

The objective of this chapter is to introduce the use of computer spreadsheets for financial modelling in leisure management. The overriding point is that spreadsheets are basically simple, logical and therefore easy to learn. The potential for spreadsheets to improve the quality of managers' work and to release time for the real issues is well worth the investment of time in learning to use them. The chapter has the following functions:

(i)   To explain, in general terms, the basics of how computer spreadsheets function;

(ii) To illustrate the benefits of computer spreadsheets to leisure managers by demonstrating a few worked examples;

(iii) To introduce the concept of the "what if" scenario and to show how managers can see the monetary effect of different conditions at the press of a button;

(iv) To examine the quantitative side of performance appraisal using computer spreadsheets.

Note: It is not possible to describe the specifics of different spreadsheet packages in this chapter. What is really important is to convey the general features that all spreadsheets are capable of. The syntax used on spreadsheet examples in this chapter can be found on the package "Framework IV". The same spreadsheet configurations will work with ALL other spreadsheets, but some of the syntax may need to be changed slightly. For example, in Framework IV we might use the command $@sum(C5:C10)$, but in Quattro Pro the same command would be $@sum(C5..C10)$. If you wish to use some of the examples and you are unsure about syntax, cither use your help menus, or consult your manuals for the finer details.

1. Computer spreadsheets

A computer spreadsheet is no more than a piece of paper with rows and columns in an electronic form. When compiling a budget manually, instinctively most of us will start by creating a grid on a piece of paper with which to organise our thoughts. A spreadsheet is much the same as a paper grid but with considerable advantages over manual methods.

The distinction between manual and computerised budgeting can be seen by understanding the following illustration using a simple salaries budget.

Manual Method

Salaries Budget	£
Centre Manager	19,000
Assistant Manager	13,000
Senior Lifeguard	12,000
Sports Instructor	12,000
Admin Assistant	10,000
Plant Supervisor	10,000
Total	76,000

Using the manual method, the total figure is calculated by adding up each line in turn, probably using a calculator.

Spreadsheet Method

	A	B
1	Centre Manager	19,000
2	Assistant Manager	13,000
3	Senior Lifeguard	12,000
4	Sports Instructor	12,000
5	Admin Assistant	10,000
6	Plant Supervisor	10,000
7		----------
8	Total	76,000 (Note 1)
9		=====

Note 1: The formula for cell B8 would be *@sum(B1:B6)* which is spreadsheet syntax for the command "add up everything from cell B1 and cell B6 inclusive". Using abbreviated syntax such as the *@sum* command is far more helpful than having to type in the alternative B1+B2+B3+B4+B5+B6 which would probably be slower than the manual method if the column was 20 or 30 rows deep.

What if?

One of the most important financial management skills for leisure managers is the ability to simulate the monetary outcomes of different scenarios. For example, the manager of a private health club should know the effects of under achieving on the budgeted number of paid-up members. This would be conducted by creating a budgeted model of the predicted level of membership either on paper or on a spreadsheet. This model could then be used to simulate the effects of differing numbers of paid-up members. This is known as a "what if" calculation.

Practical demonstration of a "what if" calculation

"What if" the pay settlement was a one-off payment to all staff of £650?

Using the manual method, a manager would probably have to write out the salaries schedule again, entering the new figures and then adding them up.

Using a spreadsheet method, the manager would simply have to overtype the existing figures with the revised salary totals. In the configuring of the spreadsheet, cell B8 has been "programmed" to calculate automatically the salary total, i.e. the sum of cells B1 to B6. In fact, if any single figure, or any combination of figures, within the specified range of cells were to be changed, then the "Total" figure in cell B8 would recalculate automatically.

	A	B
1	Centre Manager	19,650
2	Assistant Manager	13,650
3	Senior Lifeguard	12,650
4	Sports Instructor	12,650
5	Admin Assistant	10,650
6	Plant Supervisor	10,650
7		---------
8	Total	79,900 @sum(B1:B6)
9		=====

This is a simplistic use of a spreadsheet but it highlights the basic principles of how they can be used to make the production of financial information quick and accurate.

A second major advantage of spreadsheets is the ability to copy narrative, numbers or formulae from one cell to another easily and quickly. It would be rather tedious to have to type in and edit the command *@sum(B1:B6)* twelve times if you were constructing a profit and loss account for a year.

Basic steps in constructing a computer spreadsheet
Imagine that you were required to put together a month by month spreadsheet for the first six months of a financial year using the salaries above as your data. The following example shows how a spreadsheet can enable you to do this quickly and accurately.

Step 1
It is important to estimate the size of your spreadsheet prior to beginning work on it. In this example eight columns will be needed. These are required for: job title (1 column), the months April to September (6 columns) and a total (1 column).

The depth (i.e. the number of rows) will need to be at least eight but it is always worth having a few more for labelling and checking purposes.

Step 2

The basic framework or skeleton of the spreadsheet should be planned. This can be done relatively simply by defining exactly what you want to achieve. In this case, a manager would be trying to create a six month budget detailing how much each individual will earn during the period and how much the monthly wage bill will be. As an added feature, we will also build in a check to ensure that the figures agree horizontally and vertically. A typical spreadsheet outline would appear as shown in the grid below.

The outline spreadsheet below would be typical for presenting the data in this example.

	A	**B**	**C**	**D**	**E**	**F**	**G**	**H**
1	Salaries Budget							
2								
3	Job Title	April	May	June	July	Aug	Sept	Total
4								
5	Centre Manager							
6	Assistant Manager							
7	Senior Lifeguard							
8	Sports Instructor							
9	Admin Assistant							
10	Plant Supervisor							
11		------	------	------	------	------	------	------
12	Total							
13	Cumulative							
14								

The major points about the design of a spreadsheet are:

(i) Spreadsheets can contain narrative, numbers and any other characters that help to produce a professional looking document e.g. the dashes "------" at the end of each month's total.

(ii) The width of columns can be increased or decreased to suit you specific requirements. Normally this means wide columns for narrative, e.g. job titles and narrow columns for figures.

Step 3

Data can be inputted directly into the first column. Then the formula to add up this column, i.e. *@sum(B5:B10)* can be entered into cell B12. As an added bonus, each cell can act as a mini-calculator. In this example, there would be no need to perform any calculations to obtain the monthly salary for each member of staff from the annual salary figure. For the centre manager, the figure of 1638 in cell B5 could be entered as either a formula, i.e. 19650/12, or directly as the result of a manual calculation, i.e. the number 1638.

	A	B	C	D	E	F	G	H
1	Salaries Budget							
2								
3	Job Title	April	May	June	July	Aug	Sept	Total
4								
5	Centre Manager	1638						
6	Assistant Manager	1138						
7	Senior Lifeguard	1054						
8	Sports Instructor	1054						
9	Admin Assistant	888						
10	Plant Supervisor	888						
11		------	------	------	------	------	------	------
12	Total	6660						
13	Cumulative							
14								

The calculation for cell B12 is *@sum(B5:B10)*.

Step 4

By using the "copy" command, the spreadsheet can now be almost totally completed. In this example, because the data is the same for all six months, we can take a shortcut by copying the April data into the remaining columns for May to September. Where spreadsheets become exciting is in their ability to respond intelligently to copying formulae as well as numbers and narrative. To enter the formulae to calculate monthly salary totals, it is common practice to use the copy command. Having entered *@sum(B5:B10)* in cell B12, this formula can be used as the basis for the formula for the remaining monthly totals. The novice's natural reaction would be to think that copying a formula would result in the formula being copied as typed, i.e. *@sum(B5:B10)*. This is not the case. Spreadsheets demonstrate considerable power by altering formula to reflect the columns that they have been copied into. For May, *@sum(B5:B10)* would automatically be modified to *@sum(C5:C10)* and for September, *@sum(G5:G10)*. All this is achieved by entering the formula once and copying it.

Having calculated the monthly (column) totals, it is also possible to calculate the job (row) totals. In the case of the centre manager, the total amount of salary earned in the period would be calculated by entering the formula *@sum(B5:G5)* in cell H5. By copying the formula in cell H5 downwards, the spreadsheet alters the row numbers to make the formula appropriate for each row. The benefits in terms of time saved and accuracy in using the copy command compared with manual methods cannot be over-emphasised.

	A	B	C	D	E	F	G	H
1	Salaries Budget							
2								
3	Job Title	April	May	June	July	Aug	Sept	Total
4								
5	Centre Manager	1638	1638	1638	1638	1638	1638	@sum(B5:G5) 9828
6	Assistant Manager	1138	1138	1138	1138	1138	1138	6828
7	Senior Lifeguard	1054	1054	1054	1054	1054	1054	6324
8	Sports Instructor	1054	1054	1054	1054	1054	1054	6324
9	Admin Assistant	888	888	888	888	888	888	5328
10	Plant Supervisor	888	888	888	888	888	888	@sum(B10:G10) 5328
11		------	------	------	------	------	------	------
12	Total	6660	6660	6660	6660	6660	6660	39960
13	Cumulative							
14								

Step 5

The final task is to build a check into the spreadsheet which tests it for accuracy. There is a popular misconception that because spreadsheets look orderly that they are therefore correct. This is not the case and it is always worth building in a cross-check for internal accuracy. Submitting a spreadsheet to your immediate supervisor that does not work is nearly as bad as submitting nothing at all. The logic to the cross-check is simple: if the sum of the rows (H12) equals the sum of the columns (B12:G12), then the mechanics of the spreadsheet must be correct. This is tested by using the cumulative column totals.

	A	B	C	D	E	F	G	H
1	Salaries Budget							
2								
3	Job Title	April	May	June	July	Aug	Sept	Total
4								
5	Centre Manager	1638	1638	1638	1638	1638	1638	9828
6	Assistant Manager	1138	1138	1138	1138	1138	1138	6828
7	Senior Lifeguard	1054	1054	1054	1054	1054	1054	6324
8	Sports Instructor	1054	1054	1054	1054	1054	1054	6324
9	Admin Assistant	888	888	888	888	888	888	5328
10	Plant Supervisor	888	888	888	888	888	888	5328
11		-------	-------	-------	-------	-------	-------	-------
12	Total	6660	6660	6660	6660	6660	6660	39960
13	Cumulative	B12 6660	B13+C12 13320	C13+D12 19980	D13+E12 26640	E13+F12 33300	F13+G12 39960	

Even the formula in cell C13 could be copied to the other columns to complete the accuracy check even quicker. For many managers, learning to apply spreadsheets to solve real-world problems will revolutionise the way in which they work overnight.

The simple examples above have used nothing more complicated than adding up rows and columns. This is but a tiny part of the overall uses of spreadsheets. The only real limitations to what a spreadsheet can do with numbers is your imagination! A few examples include: using spreadsheets to analyse data from customer surveys; producing daily banking sheets on which you simply enter gross takings; and monitoring expenditure using a spreadsheet based control sheet. The saying "necessity is the mother of invention" could not be more apt for spreadsheets. The only way to really come to grips with them is by having to use them rather than taking part in an academic exercise. Some wider applications of spreadsheets and templates with formulae in them are shown in the next section.

A further significant application of spreadsheets is using them to "read" data from one another. As an example, having set up a monthly profit and loss account master budget, it is possible to construct other spreadsheets that are linked to this master budget. Applications include reading month only and cumulative data from the master budget to produce management accounts. This enables management accounts to be produced in a standard form and with great accuracy as it minimises the need for manual calculations. The data requirements for management and control described in Chapter 3 lend themselves to this type of spreadsheet linking. The precise details of this are illustrated in the next section of this chapter and can be adapted to suit any leisure management context.

2 Practical applications of computer spreadsheets

A major advantage of spreadsheets is that they are almost infinitely flexible in their capability for making calculations or presenting data. This fits well with the concept of management accounting, which is a usually a method of internal reporting on the financial affairs of a business. Using spreadsheets, it is possible to present data in whatever format is considered to be the most informative.

Example
Consider the case of a theatre manager who wishes to produce a budgeted monthly profit and loss account and who also wants to use this as the basis for producing budget versus actual comparisons. How could this be made to work in practice using spreadsheets?

The budgeted profit and loss account
The important features of this section are twofold: firstly, understanding the layout of a budgeted profit and loss account; and, secondly, converting this layout into a spreadsheet format. The figures which are used in the various examples are for illustrative purposes only. Therefore, developing the theatre example further, a budgeted profit and loss account in monthly format might appear as laid out in Spreadsheet 1.

#	A	B	C	D	E	F	G	H	I	J	K	L	M	N
		April	May	June	July	Aug	Sept	Oct	Nov	Dec	Jan	Feb	March	Total
1	Theatre Example - Monthly Profit & Loss Account Budget													
2														
3		April	May	June	July	Aug	Sept	Oct	Nov	Dec	Jan	Feb	March	Total
4														
5	INCOME													
6	Box Office	12150	12909	10631	9113	12909	10631	13061	13669	16706	18225	12530	11543	154077
7	Trading Operations	1823	1936	1595	1367	1936	1595	1959	2050	2506	2734	1879	1731	23112
8	Rentals	608	645	532	456	645	532	653	683	835	911	626	577	7704
9	Sponsorship	0	1000	1000	0	500	500	0	1500	1000	500	1000	1000	8000
10	Regional Arts Board	0	10000	0	0	10000	0	0	10000	0	0	10000	0	40000
11	Local Authority	15000	0	0	12000	0	0	10000	0	0	7500	0	0	44500
12	TOTAL INCOME	29580	26491	13758	22935	25991	13258	25674	27903	21048	29870	26036	14851	277393
13	Cumulative Total	29580	56071	69829	92764	118755	132013	157686	185589	206636	236506	262542	277393	277393
14														
15	EXPENDITURE													
16	SALARIES/WAGES													105825
17	Full Time Salaries	8500	8500	8500	8925	8925	8925	8925	8925	8925	8925	8925	8925	105825
18	Box Office	625	600	800	750	800	900	1000	900	1100	800	750	700	9725
19	Front of House Staff	450	500	700	600	550	800	750	600	650	725	800	500	7625
20	Cleaners	475	475	475	475	475	475	500	500	500	500	500	500	5850
21	National Insurance	1050	1053	1095	1123	1123	1160	1168	1142	1168	1144	1147	1110	13483
22	Salary Total	11100	11128	11570	11873	11873	12260	12343	12067	12343	12094	12122	11735	142508
23	Cumulative Total	11100	22228	33798	45671	57544	69804	82147	94214	106557	118651	130773	142508	142508
24														
25	PREMISES													
26	Rent/Rates/Water	815	820	840	840	700	850	2500	790	1750	750	850	1200	12705
27	Heat/Light	500	475	475	300	300	300	450	575	600	1000	1250	1200	7425
28	Cleaning Materials	150	150	150	150	150	150	150	150	150	150	150	150	1800
29	Repairs	250	75	75	300	50	50	200	100	100	300	50	50	1600
30	Total	1715	1520	1540	1590	1200	1350	3300	1615	2600	2200	2300	2600	23530
31	Cumulative Total	1715	3235	4775	6365	7565	8915	12215	13830	16430	18630	20930	23530	23530
32														
33	SUPPLIES AND SERVICES													
34	Travel/Hospitality	90	90	90	90	90	90	90	90	90	90	90	90	1080
35	Telephone	0	0	0	350	0	0	350	0	0	350	0	0	1050
36	Stationery	175	175	175	175	175	175	175	175	175	175	175	175	2100
37	Professional Fees	200	2000	175	150	200	600	130	190	200	150	125	200	4320
38	Total	465	2265	440	765	465	865	745	455	465	765	390	465	8550
39	Cumulative Total	465	2730	3170	3935	4400	5265	6010	6465	6930	7695	8085	8550	8550
40														
41	MARKETING													
42	Print & Publicity	3250	200	4000	200	3000	275	3100	500	3500	200	3000	700	21925
43	Advertising	800	684	684	684	800	684	684	684	800	684	684	684	8556
44	Other	95	95	95	95	95	95	95	95	95	95	95	95	1140
45	Total	4145	979	4779	979	3895	1054	3879	1279	4395	979	3779	1479	31621
46	Cumulative Total	4145	5124	9903	10882	14777	15831	19710	20989	25384	26363	30142	31621	31621
47														
48	PROGRAMME													
49	Artistes' Fees	4000	4250	3500	3000	4250	3500	4300	4500	5500	6000	4125	3800	50725
50	Production Costs	1400	1488	1225	1050	1488	1225	1505	1575	1925	2100	1444	1330	17754
51	Total	5400	5738	4725	4050	5738	4725	5805	6075	7425	8100	5569	5130	68479
52	Cumulative Total	5400	11138	15863	19913	25650	30375	36180	42255	49680	57780	63349	68479	68479
53														
54	TOTAL EXPENDITURE	22825	21629	23054	19257	23171	20254	26072	21491	27228	24138	24160	21409	274688
55	Cumulative Total	22825	44455	67508	86766	109936	130190	156262	177753	204981	229119	253279	274688	274688
56														
57	SUMMARY													
58	SURPLUS/(DEFICIT)	6755	4862	-9296	3678	2820	-6996	-398	6412	-6180	5732	1876	-6558	2705
59	Cumulative	6755	11617	2321	5998	8819	1822	1424	7836	1655	7387	9263	2705	2705

Spreadsheet 1

The more helpful features of this format can be summarised as follows:

(i)   The planned performance for each month can be seen clearly in isolation.

(ii) Even though the profit and loss account is presented on a monthly basis, the position for the year as a whole is also immediately obvious, i.e. a budgeted surplus of £2,705.

(iii) Income and costs have been grouped into meaningful subheadings which permit performance appraisal of discrete parts of the business, e.g. marketing or premises costs.

The same spreadsheet can now be presented in such a way as to illustrate the formulae which have been used to create it (see Spreadsheet 2).

On first appearances, Spreadsheet 2 may appear to be somewhat daunting, but closer inspection will reveal that it is all very logical and uses nothing more complicated than addition, subtraction and multiplication. To grasp fully how the budget report and the formulae spreadsheet relate to one another, it is advisable that you compare the two and identify precisely how the two grids are, in effect, the same thing expressed in different terms. This should convince you that it is considerably easier than it may appear at first.

Once the formulae for the first month have been put in place, then 75% of the work has been done. All that is needed now is to copy the first month's formula into the remaining eleven months. Similarly, once the formula for the first row in the Total column has been written, it too can be copied for the remaining rows. The spreadsheet will also pick up the pattern of the cumulative total formulae and copy these intelligently. The first month's formula is not relevant, but copying the formula for the second month will work for the remaining ten columns.

Note how under the Salaries/Wages subheading it has been possible to write a formula to calculate National Insurance costs. Currently, employers pay 10.45% in National Insurance which is an additional cost to the wages paid to employees. The formula used means that if managers wish to try some "what if" calculations on the salaries/wages, then the National Insurance cost will change automatically.

The significance of the master budget file is that it can be used as the basis for a series of integrated financial reports which will help to minimise error. Integrated in this context means that the budget reports are derived from the same basic spreadsheet only.

The month only financial report

Imagine that the manager wished to produce a financial report for the month of October. The important data is what has actually happened and what was

A	B	C	D	E	F	G	H	I	J	K	L	M	N
Theatre Example - Monthly Profit & Loss Account Budget													
	April	May	June	July	Aug	Sept	Oct	Nov	Dec	Jan	Feb	March	Total
INCOME													
Box Office													@sum(B6:M6)
Trading Operations													@sum(B7:M7)
Rentals													@sum(B8:M8)
Sponsorship													@sum(B9:M9)
Regional Arts Board													@sum(B10:M10)
Local Authority													@sum(B11:M11)
TOTAL INCOME	@sum(B11:B6)	@sum(C11:C6)	@sum(D11:D6)	@sum(E11:E6)	@sum(F11:F6)	@sum(G11:G6)	@sum(H11:H6)	@sum(I11:I6)	@sum(J11:J6)	@sum(K11:K6)	@sum(L11:L6)	@sum(M11:M6)	@sum(B12:M12)
Cumulative Total	B12	B13+C12	C13+D12	D13+E12	E13+F12	F13+G12	G13+H12	H13+I12	I13+J12	J13+K12	K13+L12	L13+M12	
EXPENDITURE													
SALARIES/WAGES													
Full Time Salaries													@sum(B17:M17)
Box Office													@sum(B18:M18)
Front of House Staff													@sum(B19:M19)
Cleaners													@sum(B20:M20)
National Insurance	@sum(B20:B17)*.1045	@sum(C20:C17)*.1045	@sum(D20:D17)*.1045	@sum(E20:E17)*.1045	@sum(F20:F17)*.1045	@sum(G20:G17)*.1045	@sum(H20:H17)*.1045	@sum(I20:I17)*.1045	@sum(J20:J17)*.1045	@sum(K20:K17)*.1045	@sum(L20:L17)*.1045	@sum(M20:M17)*.1045	@sum(B21:M21)
Salary Total	@sum(B21:B17)	@sum(C21:C17)	@sum(D21:D17)	@sum(E21:E17)	@sum(F21:F17)	@sum(G21:G17)	@sum(H21:H17)	@sum(I21:I17)	@sum(J21:J17)	@sum(K21:K17)	@sum(L21:L17)	@sum(M21:M17)	@sum(B22:M22)
Cumulative Total	B22	B23+C22	C23+D22	D23+E22	E23+F22	F23+G22	G23+H22	H23+I22	I23+J22	J23+K22	K23+L22	L23+M22	
PREMISES													
Rent/Rates/Water													@sum(B26:M26)
Heat/Light													@sum(B27:M27)
Cleaning Materials													@sum(B28:M28)
Repairs													@sum(B29:M29)
Total	@sum(B29:B26)	@sum(C29:C26)	@sum(D29:D26)	@sum(E29:E26)	@sum(F29:F26)	@sum(G29:G26)	@sum(H29:H26)	@sum(I29:I26)	@sum(J29:J26)	@sum(K29:K26)	@sum(L29:L26)	@sum(M29:M26)	@sum(B30:M30)
Cumulative Total	B30	C30+B31	D30+C31	E30+D31	F30+E31	G30+F31	H30+G31	I30+H31	J30+I31	K30+J31	L30+K31	M30+L31	
SUPPLIES AND SERVICES													
Travel/Hospitality													@sum(B34:M34)
Telephone													@sum(B35:M35)
Stationery													@sum(B36:M36)
Professional Fees													@sum(B37:M37)
Total	@sum(B37:B34)	@sum(C37:C34)	@sum(D37:D34)	@sum(E37:E34)	@sum(F37:F34)	@sum(G37:G34)	@sum(H37:H34)	@sum(I37:I34)	@sum(J37:J34)	@sum(K37:K34)	@sum(L37:L34)	@sum(M37:M34)	@sum(B38:M38)
Cumulative Total	B38	C38+B39	D38+C39	E38+D39	F38+E39	G38+F39	H38+G39	I38+H39	J38+I39	K38+J39	L38+K39	M38+L39	
MARKETING													
Print & Publicity													@sum(B42:M42)
Advertising													@sum(B43:M43)
Other													@sum(B44:M44)
Total	@sum(B44:B42)	@sum(C44:C42)	@sum(D44:D42)	@sum(E44:E42)	@sum(F44:F42)	@sum(G44:G42)	@sum(H44:H42)	@sum(I44:I42)	@sum(J44:J42)	@sum(K44:K42)	@sum(L44:L42)	@sum(M44:M42)	@sum(B45:M45)
Cumulative Total	B45	C45+B46	D45+C46	E45+D46	F45+E46	G45+F46	H45+G46	I45+H46	J45+I46	K45+J46	L45+K46	M45+L46	
PROGRAMME													
Artistes' Fees													@sum(B49:M49)
Production Costs													@sum(B50:M50)
Total	@sum(B50:B49)	@sum(C50:C49)	@sum(D50:D49)	@sum(E50:E49)	@sum(F50:F49)	@sum(G50:G49)	@sum(H50:H49)	@sum(I50:I49)	@sum(J50:J49)	@sum(K50:K49)	@sum(L50:L49)	@sum(M50:M49)	@sum(B51:M51)
Cumulative Total	B51	C51+B52	D51+C52	E51+D52	F51+E52	G51+F52	H51+G52	I51+H52	J51+I52	K51+J52	L51+K52	M51+L52	
TOTAL EXPENDITURE	B22+B30+B38+B45+B51	C22+C30+C38+C45+C51	D22+D30+D38+D45+D51	E22+E30+E38+E45+E51	F22+F30+F38+F45+F51	G22+G30+G38+G45+G51	H22+H30+H38+H45+H51	I22+I30+I38+I45+I51	J22+J30+J38+J45+J51	K22+K30+K38+K45+K51	L22+L30+L38+L45+L51	M22+M30+M38+M45+M51	@sum(B54:M54)
Cumulative Total	B54	B55+C54	C55+D54	D55+E54	E55+F54	F55+G54	G55+H54	H55+I54	I55+J54	J55+K54	K55+L54	L55+M54	
SUMMARY													
SURPLUS/(DEFICIT)	B12-B54	C12-C54	D12-D54	E12-E54	F12-F54	G12-G54	H12-H54	I12-I54	J12-J54	K12-K54	L12-L54	M12-M54	N12-N54
Cumulative	B58	B59+C58	C59+D58	D59+E58	E59+F58	F59+G58	G59+H58	H59+I58	I59+J58	J59+K58	K59+L58	L59+M58	

Spreadsheet 2

planned to happen. As the budgeted profit and loss account has already been produced, it seems sensible to use the existing work to produce the majority of the financial report. The final output might appear as in Table 5.1.

	A	B	C	D	E	F	G	H
1	Theatre Example – Typical Monthly Report							
2	Profit and Loss Account for October							
3								
4		Actual	Incurred	Total	Budget	Variance	(U/F)	Note
5	INCOME							
6	Box Office	13200		13200	13061	−139	F	1
7	Trading Operations	2100		2100	1959	−141	F	1
8	Rentals	700		700	653	−47	F	1
9	Sponsorship	0		0	0	0	−	
10	Regional Arts Board	0		0	0	0	−	
11	Local Authority	10000		10000	10000	0	−	
12	TOTAL INCOME	26000	0	26000	25674	−327	F	
13								
14	EXPENDITURE							
15	SALARIES/WAGES							
16	Full Time Salaries	8900	8900	8925	25	F		
17	Box Office	950	950	1000	50	F		
18	Front of House Staff	770	770	750	−20	U		
19	Cleaners	525	525	500	−25	U		
20	National Insurance	1112	1112	116	56	F		
21	Salary Total	12257	0	12257	12343	86	F	
22								
23								
24	PREMISES							
25	Rent/Rates/Water	2659		2659	2500	−159	U	2
26	Heat/Light	525		525	450	−75	U	
27	Cleaning Materials	170	50	220	150	−70	U	
28	Repairs	180		180	200	20	F	
29	Total	3534	50	3584	3300	−284	U	
30								
31								
32	SUPPLIES AND SERVICES							
33	Travel/Hospitality	110		110	90	−20	U	
34	Telephone	275		275	350	75	F	
35	Stationery	135		135	175	40	F	
36	Professional Fees	0	125	125	130	5	F	
37	Total	520	125	645	745	100	F	
38								
39								
40	MARKETING							
41	Print & Publicity	2500	575	3075	3100	25	F	
42	Advertising	700	700	684	−16	U		
43	Other	40	40	95	55	F		
44	Total	3240	575	3815	3879	64	F	
45								
46								
47	PROGRAMME							
48	Artistes' Fees	4125		4125	4300	175	F	3
49	Production Costs	1625		1625	1505	−120	U	3
50	Total	5750	0	5750	5805	55	F	
51								
52								
53	TOTAL EXPENDITURE	25301	750	26051	26072	21	F	
54								
55								
56	SUMMARY							
57	SURPLUS/(DEFICIT)	699	−750	−51	−398	−347	F	4

Table 5.1

The technique and the formula used to create this report are relatively simple. The major point of note is that the budget figures have been read directly out of the master budget (MB) file. Converted into spreadsheet format the report in Table 5.1 would appear as shown in Spreadsheet 3.

	A	B	C	D	E	F	G	H
1	Theatre Example Profit and Loss Account for October							
2	Spreadsheet Format							
3								
4		Actual	Incurred	Total	Budget	Variance	(U/F)	Note
5	INCOME							
6	Box Office			B6+C6	MB.H6	E6-D6		
7	Trading Operations			B7+C7	MB.H7	E7-D7		
8	Rentals			B8+C8	MB.H8	E8-D8		
9	Sponsorship			B9+C9	MB.H9	E9-D9		
10	Regional Arts Board			B10+C10	MB.H10	E10-D10		
11	Local Authority			B11+C11	MB.H11	E11-D11		
12	TOTAL INCOME	@sum(B11:B6)	@sum(C11:C6)	@sum(D11:D6)	MB.H12	@sum(F11:F6)		
13								
14								
15	EXPENDITURE							
16	SALARIES/WAGES							
17	Full Time Salaries				MB.H17	E17-D17		
18	Box Office				MB.H18	E18-D18		
19	Front of House Staff				MB.H19	E19-D19		
20	Cleaners				MB.H20	E20-D20		
21	National Insurance				MB.H21	E21-D21		
22	Salary Total	@sum(B21:B17)	@sum(C21:C17)	@sum(D21:D17)	MB.H22	@sum(F21:F17)		
23								
24								
25	PREMISES							
26	Rent/Rates/Water				MB.H26	E26-D26		
27	Heat/Light				MB.H27	E27-D27		
28	Cleaning Materials				MB.H28	E28-D28		
29	Repairs				MB.H29	E29-D29		
30	Total	@sum(B29:B26)	@sum(C29:C26)	@sum(D29:D26)	MB.H30	@sum(F29:F26)		
31								
32								
33	SUPPLIES AND SERVICES							
34	Travel/Hospitality				MB.H34	E34-D34		
35	Telephone				MB.H35	E35-D35		
36	Stationery				MB.H36	E36-D36		
37	Professional Fees				MB.H37	E37-D37		
38	Total	@sum(B37:B34)	@sum(C37:C34)	@sum(D37:D34)	MB.H38	@sum(F37:F34)		
39								
40								
41	MARKETING							
42	Print & Publicity				MB.H42	E42-D42		
43	Advertising				MB.H43	E43-D43		
44	Other				MB.H44	E44-D44		
45	Total	@sum(B44:B42)	@sum(C44:C42)	@sum(D44:D42)	MB.H45	@sum(F44:F42)		
46								
47								
48	PROGRAMME							
49	Artistes' Fees				MB.H49	E49-D49		
50	Production Costs				MB.H50	E50-D50		
51	Total	@sum(B50:B49)	@sum(C50:C49)	@sum(D50:D49)	MB.H51	@sum(F50:F49)		
52								
53								
54	TOTAL EXPENDITURE	B22+B30+B38+B45+B51	C22+C30+C38+C45+C51	D22+D30+D38+D45+D51	MB.H54	E54-D54		
55								
56								
57	SUMMARY							
58	SURPLUS/(DEFICIT)	B12-B54	C12-C54	D12-D54	MB.H58	E58-D58		

Spreadsheet 3

It is essential that the concept of linking spreadsheets to one another is understood in order to make a system of this type work. From a management point of view, once the basic template has been created, the only figures which need to be entered manually are those in the "actual" column. The efficiency and ease of this type of system enables managers to present budget reports quickly and accurately. Their work focus can now be on controlling the business rather than dreaming up a new type of budget report every month. Arguably, the most important budget statement is the cumulative or "to date" report. This too uses the same principles to produce meaningful data.

The cumulative financial report

In addition to knowing what has happened to date compared with what was planned, the cumulative report should also provide additional data to complete the picture of the fortunes of a business. Examples include data such as the amount of budget remaining, the total budget and a forecast of what management believe will happen as a result of current performance.

	A	B	C	D	E	F	G	H	I	J	K
1	Theatre Example – Typical Monthly Report										
2	Profit and Loss Account from April to October										
3									Residual	Total	Year End
4		Actual	Incurred	Total	Budget	Variance	(U/F)	Note	Budget	Budget	Forecast
5	INCOME										
6	Box Office	82350		82350	81405	–945	F	1	72672	154077	160000
7	Trading Operations	13258		13258	12211	–1047	F	1	10901	23112	25000
8	Rentals	4235		4235	4070	–165	F	1	3634	7704	8000
9	Sponsorship	2750		2750	3000	250	U		5000	8000	6000
10	Regional Arts Board	20000		20000	20000	0	–		20000	40000	40000
11	Local Authority	37000		37000	37000	0	–		7500	44500	44500
12	TOTAL INCOME	159593	0	159593	157686	–1907	F		119707	277393	283500
13											
14											
15	EXPENDITURE										
16	SALARIES/WAGES										
17	Full Time Salaries	61395		61395	61200	–195	U	2	44625	105825	106000
18	Box Office	5498		5498	5475	–23	U		4250	9725	10500
19	Front of House Staff	4275		4275	4350	75	F		3275	7625	8000
20	Cleaners	3523		3523	3350	–173	U		2500	5850	6000
21	National Insurance	7750		7750	7772	22	F		5711	13483	13500
22	Salary Total	82441	0	82441	82147	–294	U		60361	142508	144000
23											
24											
25	PREMISES										
26	Rent/Rates/Water	7290		7290	7365	75	F		5340	12705	13000
27	Heat/Light	2857		2857	2800	–57	U		4625	7425	7000
28	Cleaning Materials	1090	50	1140	1050	–90	U		750	1800	2000
29	Repairs	987		987	1000	13	F		600	1600	1500
30	Total	12224	50	12274	12215	–59	U		11315	23530	23500
31											
32											
33	SUPPLIES AND SERVICES										
34	Travel/Hospitality	670		670	630	–40	U		450	1080	1250
35	Telephone	680		680	700	20	F		350	1050	1250
36	Stationery	1196		1196	1225	29	F		875	2100	2000
37	Professional Fees	3250	125	3375	3455	80	F		865	4320	4500
38	Total	5796	125	5921	6010	89	F		2540	8550	9000
39											
40											
41	MARKETING										
42	Print & Publicity	13656	575	14231	14025	–206	U	3	7900	21925	23000
43	Advertising	4978		4978	5020	42	F		3536	8556	9000
44	Other	725		725	665	–60	U		475	1140	1200
45	Total	19359	575	19934	19710	–224	U		11911	31621	33200
46											
47											
48	PROGRAMME										
49	Artistes' Fees	25900		25900	26800	900	F	4	23925	50725	51000
50	Production Costs	10398		10398	9380	–1018	U	4	8374	17754	18000
51	Total	36298	0	36298	36180	–118	U		32299	68479	69000
52											
53											
54	TOTAL EXPENDITURE	156118	750	156868	156262	–606	U		118426	274688	278700
55											
56											
57	SUMMARY										
58	SURPLUS/(DEFICIT)	3475	–750	2725	1424	–1301	F	5	1281	2705	4800

Table 5.2

The principles involved in producing a budget report such as the one in Table 5.2 are much the same as for the monthly report, but modified slightly and expanded to meet the increased data requirements. The important point of note is to reinforce how the same basic data and structure are being reused. For different months, all that the person in charge of producing these reports has to do is to change the formulae (using the "copy" function) and to enter the actual figures. A simple system such as this requires some thought and investment of time during the setting up phases but the benefits in terms of accuracy and time saving are well worth it. The formulae themselves are illustrated in Table 5.3.

Hopefully, having shattered the myth that the use of spreadsheets requires computer programming skills, managers will realise that by using nothing more complicated than you would find on a calculator, spreadsheets do have a relevance to the leisure industry.

3 The "what if" scenario revisited

The use of spreadsheets is not confined to the monitoring and review stages of the budget cycle. They can also play an important role in the construction of budgets by enabling the basic modelling or simulation of different scenarios. Obviously this is possible using the manual method. It is, however, tedious to rewrite a paper example every time that you look at an alternative set of conditions. There are endless permutations for "what if" calculations. However, the ones which are most commonly used are either on an individual component of the budget (e.g. wages), or on the budget as a whole (e.g. 5% increase in admissions). In recognition of this, two examples illustrating each type of "what if" scenario are modelled below with their accompanying spreadsheets.

Example: simple wages example

A sports centre has a full-time staff of eight who are contracted to an annually negotiated pay rise between management and unions. Normally the settlement is not made prior to the start of the financial year and the first draft of the budget can at best be described as a "guestimate". Clearly, it is not possible to solve this problem but it is possible to simulate a best case, most probable case and worst case scenario using a spreadsheet. Assume these to be 2%, 4% and 6% respectively.

Sports centre wages budget: best case scenario – 2% wage increase

Position	Current Salary	Increase Factor	Next Year's Salary
Centre Manager	18,525	2.00%	18,896
Assistant Manager	15,345	2.00%	15,652
Duty Manager 1	14,650	2.00%	14,943
Duty Manager 2	14,325	2.00%	14,612
Pool Supervisor	12,185	2.00%	12,429
PA/Secretary	11,985	2.00%	12,225
Sports Coach	11,450	2.00%	11,679
Maintenance Person	10,985	2.00%	11,205
Totals	109,450		111,639

#	A	B	C	D	E	F	G	H	I	J	K
1	Profit and Loss Account from April to October										
2											
3									Residual	Total	Year End
4		Actual	Incurred	Total	Budget	Variance	(U/F)	Note	Budget	Budget	Forecast
5	INCOME										
6	Box Office			B6+C6	@SUM(MB.B6:MB.H6)	E6-D6			MB.N6-E6	MB.N6	
7	Trading Operations			B7+C7	@SUM(MB.B7:MB.H7)	E7-D7			MB.N7-E7	MB.N7	
8	Rentals			B8+C8	@SUM(MB.B8:MB.H8)	E8-D8			MB.N8-E8	MB.N8	
9	Sponsorship			B9+C9	@SUM(MB.B9:MB.H9)	E9-D9			MB.N9-E9	MB.N9	
10	Regional Arts Board			B10+C10	@SUM(MB.B10:MB.H10)	E10-D10			MB.N10-E10	MB.N10	
11	Local Authority			B11+C11	@SUM(MB.B11:MB.H11)	E11-D11			MB.N11-E11	MB.N11	
12	TOTAL INCOME	@SUM(B6:B11)	@SUM(C6:C11)	@SUM(D6:D11)	@SUM(MB.B12:MB.H12)	@SUM(F6:F11)			MB.N12-E12	MB.N12	@sum(K11:K6)
13											
14											
15	EXPENDITURE										
16	SALARIES/WAGES										
17	Full Time Salaries			B17+C17	@SUM(MB.B17:MB.H17)	E17-D17			MB.N17-E17	MB.N17	
18	Box Office			B18+C18	@SUM(MB.B18:MB.H18)	E18-D18			MB.N18-E18	MB.N18	
19	Front of House Staff			B19+C19	@SUM(MB.B19:MB.H19)	E19-D19			MB.N19-E19	MB.N19	
20	Cleaners			B20+C20	@SUM(MB.B20:MB.H20)	E20-D20			MB.N20-E20	MB.N20	
21	National Insurance			B21+C21	@SUM(MB.B21:MB.H21)	E21-D21			MB.N21-E21	MB.N21	
22	Salary Total	@SUM(B17:B21)	@SUM(C17:C21)	@SUM(D17:D21)	@SUM(MB.B22:MB.H22)	@SUM(F17:F21)			MB.N22-E22	MB.N22	@sum(K21:K17)
23											
24											
25	PREMISES										
26	Rent/Rates/Water			B26+C26	@SUM(MB.B26:MB.H26)	E26-D26			MB.N26-E26	MB.N26	
27	Heat/Light			B27+C27	@SUM(MB.B27:MB.H27)	E27-D27			MB.N27-E27	MB.N27	
28	Cleaning Materials			B28+C28	@SUM(MB.B28:MB.H28)	E28-D28			MB.N28-E28	MB.N28	
29	Repairs			B29+C29	@SUM(MB.B29:MB.H29)	E29-D29			MB.N29-E29	MB.N29	
30	Total	@SUM(B26:B29)	@SUM(C26:C29)	@SUM(D26:D29)	@SUM(MB.B30:MB.H30)	@SUM(F26:F29)			MB.N30-E30	MB.N30	@sum(K26:K26)
31											
32											
33	SUPPLIES AND SERVICES										
34	Travel/Hospitality			B34+C34	@SUM(MB.B34:MB.H34)	E34-D34			MB.N34-E34	MB.N34	
35	Telephone			B35+C35	@SUM(MB.B35:MB.H35)	E35-D35			MB.N35-E35	MB.N35	
36	Stationery			B36+C36	@SUM(MB.B36:MB.H36)	E36-D36			MB.N36-E36	MB.N36	
37	Professional Fees			B37+C37	@SUM(MB.B37:MB.H37)	E37-D37			MB.N37-E37	MB.N37	
38	Total	@SUM(B34:B37)	@SUM(C34:C37)	@SUM(D34:D37)	@SUM(MB.B38:MB.H38)	@SUM(F34:F37)			MB.N38-E38	MB.N38	@sum(K37:K34)
39											
40											
41	MARKETING										
42	Print & Publicity			B42+C42	@SUM(MB.B42:MB.H42)	E42-D42			MB.N42-E42	MB.N42	
43	Advertising			B43+C43	@SUM(MB.B43:MB.H43)	E43-D43			MB.N43-E43	MB.N43	
44	Other			B44+C44	@SUM(MB.B44:MB.H44)	E44-D44			MB.N44-E44	MB.N44	
45	Total	@SUM(B42:B44)	@SUM(C42:C44)	@SUM(D42:D44)	@SUM(MB.B45:MB.H45)	@SUM(F42:F44)			MB.N45-E45	MB.N45	@sum(K44:K42)
46											
47											
48	PROGRAMME										
49	Artistes' Fees			B49+C49	@SUM(MB.B49:MB.H49)	E49-D49			MB.N49-E49	MB.N49	
50	Production Costs			B50+C50	@SUM(MB.B50:MB.H50)	E50-D50			MB.N50-E50	MB.N50	
51	Total	@SUM(B49:B50)	@SUM(C49:C50)	@SUM(D49:D50)	@SUM(MB.B51:MB.H51)	@SUM(F49:F50)			MB.N51-E51	MB.N45	@sum(K50:K49)
52											
53											
54	TOTAL EXPENDITURE	B22+B30+B38+B45+B51	C22+C30+C38+C45+C51	D22+D30+D38+D45+D51	@SUM(MB.B54:MB.H54)	E54-D54			MB.N54-E54	MB.N54	K22+K30+K38+K45+K51
55											
56											
57	SUMMARY										
58	SURPLUS/(DEFICIT)	B12-B54	C12-C54	D12-D54	@SUM(MB.B58:MB.H58)	E58-D58			MB.N58-E58	MB.N58	K12-K54

Table 5.3

	A	B	C	D
1	Sports Centre Wages Budget			
2	Best Case Scenario – 2% wage increase			
3				
4		Current Salary	Increase Factor	Next Year's Salary
5	Position			
6				
7	Centre Manager	18,525	2%	B7*(1+C7)
8	Assistant Manager	15,345	2%	B8*(1+C8)
9	Duty Manager 1	14,650	2%	B9*(1+C9)
10	Duty Manager 2	14,325	2%	B10*(1+C10)
11	Pool Supervisor	12,185	2%	B11*(1+C11)
12	PA/Secretary	11,985	2%	B12*(1+C12)
13	Sports Coach	11,450	2%	B13*(1+C13)
14	Maintenance Person	10,985	2%	B14*(1+C14)
15	Totals	@sum(B14:B7)		@sum(D14:D7)

By changing the percentage in the increase factor column it is possible to examine the effect of the three increase factors assumed.

Wages Budget	Best	Probable	Worst
Increase Factor	2%	4%	6%
Budgeted Cost	£111,639	£113,828	£116,017
Current Cost	£109,450	£109,450	£109,450
Increase	+2,189	+3,378	+6,567

This provides the manager with a margin in which to work and with which to examine the effects elsewhere in the budget. Often this simple sort of exercise does not happen because managers are frightened of the results. It is far more rational to have the information and be in a position to control a business, than it is to be like an ostrich with your head buried in the sand!

Example: full budget example
Once an agreed master budget has been approved, it is possible to model the effects of providing differing levels of service, for example, seeing the effects of lower or greater than planned for admissions. This is exactly the same as sensitivity analysis discussed in Chapter 4. The point of this exercise is to show how easy the process is using computer spreadsheets. Using the ten pin bowling alley example from Chapter 2, it is possible to model the effect of a –10%, –5%, +5% and +10% variation in admissions, as in Spreadsheet 4.

	A	B	C	D	E	F	G
1	Ten Pin Bowling Alley						
2	"What if" Analysis						
3							
4							
5		Average			Base		
6		Spend/Head	–10%	–5%	Case	5%	10%
7	INCOME		46800	49400	52000	54600	57200
8			----------	----------	----------	----------	----------
9							
10	Entrance Fees	£0.60	28080	29640	31200	32760	34320
11	Shoe Hire	£0.50	23400	24700	26000	27300	28600
12	Bowling Fees	£2.50	117000	123500	130000	136500	143000
13	Cafe Income	£0.90	42120	44460	46800	49140	51480
14			----------	----------	----------	----------	----------
15	Total Income	£4.50	210600	222300	234000	245700	257400
16							
17	EXPENDITURE						
18							
19	Cost of Sales	£1.25	58500	61750	65000	68250	71500
20			----------	----------	----------	----------	----------
21	Gross Profit		152100	160550	169000	177450	185900
22			----------	----------	----------	----------	----------
23							
24	Salaries		24000	24000	24000	24000	24000
25	Wages		52000	52000	52000	52000	52000
26	Premises		21000	21000	21000	21000	21000
27	Supplies		12000	12000	12000	12000	12000
28	Marketing		32500	32500	32500	32500	32500
29			----------	----------	----------	----------	----------
30	Sub Total		141500	141500	141500	141500	141500
31			----------	----------	----------	----------	----------
32							
33	NET PROFIT/(LOSS)		10600	19050	27500	35950	44400
34			=====	=====	=====	=====	=====

Spreadsheet 4

The important point of note here is to divide the incomes and expenditures into those which change in direct proportion to the number of admissions (variable costs), and those which do not change in the short term (fixed costs). These can be linked to the key variables (in this case number of admissions) to model the effects of different business conditions. As with all of the spreadsheet examples, you are advised to identify the links between the output example and the formulae in the template (see Spreadsheet 5).

	A	B	C	D	E	F	G
1	Ten Pin Bowling Alley						
2	"What if" Analysis						
3							
4							
5					Base		
6		Average	−10%	−5%	Case	5%	10%
7		Spend/Head	E7*.9	E7*.95	52000	E7*1.05	E7*1.1
8	Income	----------	----------	----------	----------	----------	----------
9							
10	Entrance Fees	0.6	C7*B10	D7*B10	E7*B10	F7*B10	G7*B10
11	Shoe Hire	0.5	C7*B11	D7*B11	E7*B11	F7*B11	G7*B11
12	Bowling Fees	2.5	C7*B12	D7*B12	E7*B12	F7*B12	G7*B12
13	Cafe Income	0.9	C7*B13	D7*B13	E7*B13	F7*B13	G7*B13
14		----------	----------	----------	----------	----------	----------
15	Total Income	4.5	0	0	0	0	0
16							
17	EXPENDITURE						
18							
19	Cost of Sales	1.25	C7*B19	D7*B19	E7*B19	F7*B19	G7*B19
20		----------	----------	----------	----------	----------	----------
21	Gross Profit		C15-C19	D15-D19	E15-E19	F15-F19	G15-G19
22		----------	----------	----------	----------	----------	----------
23							
24	Salaries		24000	24000	24000	24000	24000
25	Wages		52000	52000	52000	52000	52000
26	Premises		21000	21000	21000	21000	21000
27	Supplies		12000	12000	12000	12000	12000
28	Marketing		35200	32500	32500	32500	32500
29		----------	----------	----------	----------	----------	----------
30	Sub Total		141500	141500	141500	141500	141500
31	------------	----------	----------	----------	----------	----------	
32							
33	NET PROFIT/(LOSS)		C21-C30	D21-D30	E21-E30	F21-F30	G21-G30
34		======	======	======	======	======	

Spreadsheet 5

Once a model of this type has been created it becomes possible to model any percentage increase or decrease in admissions. One of the essential pieces of information that a manager might require is, "at what point does the business break even". The use of trial and error on a spreadsheet model will soon give an accurate answer.

The ability to model financial information accurately and quickly is one of the fundamental principles of financial control. It is naive to assume that what we have planned to happen in a year's time will occur automatically. There will inevitably be times where budgets and reality do not coincide. Rather than wait for given scenarios to occur prior to doing anything, the good manager should have pre-empted certain scenarios and have the answers ready. The best way of doing this is by using computer spreadsheets.

4 Spreadsheets and performance appraisal

A further application of the spreadsheet is to use it in the calculation of quantitative performance indicators. Obviously not all measures of performance can be quantified, e.g. number of complaints, but those which can, e.g. recovery rate, lend themselves to spreadsheet analysis.

To illustrate the basic points consider the examples of a private sector organisation (Spreadsheets 6 and 7) and a public sector organisation (Spreadsheets 8 and 9).

The use of quantitative performance indicators in this example shows absolutely clearly not only how much the performance differs from what was planned, but also how the variations can be explained.

If there is a basic point to emerge from this data, then it is to demonstrate that performance measures can be calculated from information which is being produced as a matter of course, i.e. no extra work is involved.

Public sector managers are often interested in what percentage of income or expenditure each item is responsible for. In the example here, it can be seen that 75% of expenditure is accounted for by salaries and programme. These can now be deduced as being as being the business essentials and thus this is what managers should focus their control on.

	A	B	C	D	E
1	Private Sector				
2	Ten Pin Bowling Alley				
3					
4		Actual	Budget	Variance	U/F
5					
6	Admissions	4200	4000	−200	F
7		--------	--------	--------	----
8	INCOME				
9	Entrance	2100	2400	300	U
10	Shoe Hire	1890	2000	110	U
11	Bowling	12180	10000	−2180	F
12	Cafe	4620	3600	−1020	F
13		--------	--------	--------	----
14	Total Income	20790	18000	−2790	F
15					
16	EXPENDITURE				
17					
18	Cost of Sales	5040	5000	−40	U
19					
20	Gross Profit	15750	13000	−2750	F
21		--------	--------	--------	----
22					
23	Salaries	2000	2000	0	−
24	Wages	4950	4333	−617	U
25	Premises	1750	1750	0	−
26	Supplies	1000	1000	0	−
27	Marketing	3500	2708	−792	U
28	Sub Total	13200	11791	−1409	U
29					
30	NET PROFIT/(LOSS)	2550	1209	−1341	F
31		====	====	====	==
32					
33	Return on Sales	12.27%	6.72%	−5.55%	F
34					
35	Spend per Head				
36					
37	Entrance	0.5	0.6	0.10	U
38	Shoe hire	0.45	0.5	0.05	U
39	Bowling	2.9	2.5	(0.40)	F
40	Cafe	1.1	0.9	(0.20)	F
41		--------	--------	--------	----
42	Total	4.95	4.5	(0.45)	F
43					
44	Gross Profit %	75.76%	72.22%	−3.54%	F
45	Cost of Sales	24.24%	27.78%	3.54%	F
46					
47		100.00%	100.00%	0.00%	−

Spreadsheet 6

	A	B	C	D	E
		Actual	Budget	Variance	U/F
1	Private Sector				
2	Ten Pin Bowling Alley				
3					
4		Actual	Budget	Variance	U/F
5					
6	Admissions	4200	4000	C6-B6	F
7		--------	--------	--------	----
8	INCOME				
9	Entrance	2100	C6*.6	C9-B9	U
10	Shoe Hire	1890	C6*.5	C10-B10	U
11	Bowling	12180	C6*2.5	C11-B11	F
12	Cafe	4620	C6*.9	C12-B12	F
13		--------	--------	--------	----
14	Total Income	@sum(B12:B9)	@sum(C12:C9)	C14-B14	F
15					
16	EXPENDITURE				
17					
18	Cost of Sales	5040	C6*1.25	C18-B18	U
19					
20	Gross Profit	B14-B18	C14-C18	C20-B20	F
21		--------	--------	--------	----
22					
23	Salaries	2000	2000	C23-B23	–
24	Wages	4950	4333	C24-B24	U
25	Premises	1750	1750	C25-B25	–
26	Supplies	1000	1000	C26-B26	–
27	Marketing	3500	2708	C27-B27	U
28	Sub Total	13200	@sum(C27:C23)	C28-B28	U
29					
30	NET PROFIT/(LOSS)	B20-B28	C20-C28	C30-B30	F
31		====	====	====	==
32					
33	Return on Sales	(B30/B14*100	(C30/C14)*100	C33-B33	F
34					
35	Spend per Head				
36					
37	Entrance	B9/B6	C9/C6	C37-B37	U
38	Shoe hire	B10/B6	C10/C6	C38-B38	U
39	Bowling	B11/B6	C11/C6	C39-B39	F
40	Cafe	B12/B6	C12/C6	C40-B40	F
41		--------	--------	--------	----
42	Total	@sum(B40:B37)	@sum(C40:C37)	C42-B42	F
43					
44	Gross Profit %	(B20/B14)*100	(C20/C14)*100	C44-B44	F
45	Cost of Sales	(B18/B14)*100	(C18/C14)*100	C45-B45	F
46					
47		B45+B44	C45+C44	D45+D44	–

Spreadsheet 7

	A	B	C
1	Public Sector		
2	Theatre Example		
3			
4	INCOME	Total	Per cent
5	Box Office	150000	55.05%
6	Trading Operations	23000	8.44%
7	Rentals	7000	2.57%
8	Sponsorship	8000	2.94%
9	Regional Arts Board	40000	14.68%
10	Local Authority	44500	16.33%
11		-------	-------
12	TOTAL INCOME	272500	100.00%
13			
14	EXPENDITURE		
15	Salaries	140000	51.38%
16	Premises	23850	8.75%
17	Supplies & Services	8550	3.14%
18	Marketing	31621	11.60%
19	Programme	68479	25.13%
20			
21	TOTAL EXPENDITURE	272500	100.00%
22			
23	SUMMARY		
24	SURPLUS/DEFICIT	0	
25			
26	PERFORMANCE		
27			
28	Net Expenditure	84500	
29			
30	Recovery Rate	68.99%	
31	Subsidy Rate	31.01%	
32			
33	Gross Profit	81521	
34	Gross Profit %	54.35%	

Spreadsheet 8

	A	B	C
1	Public Sector		
2	Theatre Exanple		
3			
4	INCOME	Total	Per cent
5	Box Office	150000	B5/B12
6	Trading Operations	23000	B6/B12
7	Rentals	7000	B7/B12
8	Sponsorship	8000	B8/B12
9	Regional Arts Board	40000	B9/B12
10	Local Authority	44500	B10/B12
11		--------	--------
12	TOTAL INCOME	@sum(B10:B5)	@sum(C10:C5)
13			
14	EXPENDITURE		
15	Salaries	140000	B15/B21
16	Premises	23850	B16/B21
17	Supplies & Services	8550	B17/B21
18	Marketing	31621	B18/B21
19	Programme	68479	B19/B21
20		--------	--------
21	TOTAL EXPENDITURE	((B8+B7+B6+B5)/B21)*100	@sum(C19:C15)
22			
23	SUMMARY		
24	SURPLUS/DEFICIT	B12–B21	
25			
26	PERFORMANCE		
27			
28	Net Expenditure	B21–(B8+B7+B6+B5)	
29			
30	Recovery Rate	((B8+B7+B6+B5)/B21)*100	
31	Subsidy Rate	((B9+B10)/B21)*100	
32			
33	Gross Profit	B5–B19	
34	Gross Profit %	(B33/B5)*100	

Spreadsheet 9

Notes:

(1) Net expenditure equals total expenditure minus earned income, i.e. total income minus grants or other subsidies.

(2) Recovery rate equals the percentage of total expenditure which is covered by earned income.

(3) The subsidy rate equals the percentage of income which is made up from subsidies and will obviously equal 100% – Recovery Rate.

Summary

Having read and understood this chapter, you should have an overview of the basic principles involved in using spreadsheets. The material used in this chapter has been based on real life applications of spreadsheets in the leisure industry. The various spreadsheet layouts are not meant to be prescriptive but rather a flavour of their capabilities. The best way to use spreadsheets is to use them to solve problems of your own. The aim of this chapter has been to demonstrate their simplicity and to point you in the right direction.

Review and managment applications

Having seen some of the benefits that using computer spreadsheets can bring to leisure management, consider the following questions and discussion points:

(1) How much time do you spend putting figures together? How much time do you spend controlling your business on the basis of the information provided by your budget reports?

(2) Do you have access to a personal computer with spreadsheet programme? Do you use it to help you with your financial management?

(3) Do you prepare budgets for different "what if" scenarios? Can you see the benefits of financial modelling using computer spreadsheets?

(4) What are you key quantitative performance indicators? How do you calculate them?

(5) If you are not currently using computer spreadsheets as part of your regular routine, do you feel that you are missing out on a valuable management skill?

Further reading

It is difficult to suggest specific texts for learning how to use spreadsheets. The best way to learn is to use the on-screen tutorials, help menus and manuals which are an integral part of all industry standard spreadsheet packages.